TEN MYTHS YOU MAY HEAR AT CHURCH THIS SUNDAY

RICHARD A. HENDRIX

outskirtspress

DENVER, COLORADO

CONTENTS

FOREWORD

I am not an ordained minister. Furthermore, I'm not an ordained anything: pastor, deacon, priest, reverend, elder, and am certainly not a Holy Father. I've never been to seminary nor have I studied the Greek, Hebrew, or Aramaic languages. Clearly I'm not a theologian in the strictest sense. And yet, I feel compelled to write a theological book. You may ask what would qualify me to write such a treatise when my educational training was in Finance and my career in Logistics and Transportation. Hear me out and allow me to prove that I am capable of providing insights into Scripture and some practical teaching that may change the reader's view of the Bible and today's church.

I became a believer at age 16 and, throughout my life, have been blessed to be under the tutelage of some of the finest pastors of our generation. Dr. Charles Q. Carter, Dr. Dwight "Ike" Reighard, Dr. Ken Alford, and Dr. James Merritt are but a few of my pastors in 45 years of attending primarily Baptist churches. And while I don't wish to attribute anything that appears in this book to any of them without their permission, I will gratefully say that these men taught me to read Scripture, to digest its meaning, and to apply its truth to my life. While their styles were different their message was the same. The Bible is the inspired, holy Word of God. In short, everybody ought to read it and believe it.

I have been privileged to teach weekly Bible study lessons for the better part of 40 years. That, in and of itself, does not make me an expert on the Bible or any other subject. However, by developing hundreds of Bible lessons through the years, I have had the privilege to read the Bible over and over again. Likewise, a lifetime of hearing sermons, lectures and discourses on Scripture from many of the world's most renowned spiritual minds has afforded me many diverse and substantive insights. My thirst for the knowledge that God's word provides has been one of the driving forces of my life. I have studied, quoted, cross-referenced, debated, and generally been bathed in the teachings of the Bible. I am not a novice when speaking about what the Bible says.

There is also another benefit of not being the leader of any church or denomination. I answer only to God (and secondarily the readers) when I write this book. I have the privilege of exploring the Scripture and presenting spiritual truth without fear of a backlash from any person or group. I have found, through the years, that many pastors are unwilling to delve deeply into what the Bible really says for fear of offending the deacon board, the elder committee, other pastors, the denominational leaders, or even Ms. Shirley who is 86 years old and has believed the same thing all of her life.

Let me state at the outset of this writing that the purpose of this book is not to convince you there is a God. Psalm 19:1 reads: "The heavens declare the glory of God, and the sky above proclaims his handiwork." Does it take more faith to believe in "intelligent design", a galaxy and everything in it was created by a holy and powerful God or to believe that man evolved from sludge in a world that was created by a massive explosion that cannot be explained? That the earth is exactly the right distance from the sun and all other planets to have four weather seasons, 24 hour days and 365 ¼ days in one rotation around the sun because God chose it so or because of this massive explosion? That our kidneys, stomach, heart, lungs, liver, and dozens of other vital organs function perfectly together to keep most of us healthy and active throughout life was an act of God or somehow human's evolved to this stature? When carefully examining the order and beauty of the universe, the majesty of physics, chemistry and geometry, and the power of nature's marvelous workings, even the most skeptical would have to wonder how such order came from such chaos. I trust all of my readers believe in a Supreme Being.

This book is not about reigniting wars between denominations or in any branches of the Christian church. You will notice that there is nothing here about infant baptism, eternal security, Mary's lifetime virginity, baptism by immersion, sprinkling, dunking, or pouring; in fact, there is little here about baptism at all. Stated plainly (with tongue-in-cheek), this book may aggravate some in Presbyterian, Methodist, Baptist, Catholic, Pentecostal, Church of God, and most other churches you can name. But aggravating those seeking truth is not the purpose. However, I have seen a trend that has grown for decades and is stronger now than ever before. The trend: teaching tradition or what some author or preacher says instead of delving deeply into the Word of God and teaching Scripture as veracity. Every chapter in this book deals with subjects I have heard taught in churches dozens of times through the years. Yet, none of them have a solid Biblical basis. It's time to stop and evaluate some of the ideas being taught as fact using the Bible as the measuring tool.

Ten Myths You May Hear at Church This Sunday was not written to be sensational or provocative. It is not a theological treatise meant to be substituted for the Bible as individuals search for what they believe. I am certain that some of the subject matter will put-off or offend some people. I challenge the reader before making any judgments to read carefully what is being said. To the best of your ability, lay aside pre-conceived ideas about the topics covered and let God's Word speak to you on each subject. This may mean changing your views on teachings you've heard all through life. Check carefully the

Scripture references and make sure this author has backed up his suppositions with carefully noted Biblical positions. Pray that God will help you to know the truth of His Word just as He gave it to us without the filter of any human being's opinions. Let this book guide you to a new love and appreciation of God's truth and His Holy Word.

I am challenging every reader to dedicate time for consistent and thorough Bible reading. Furthermore, test every speaker's comments and every author's book against the Word of God. Many theologians, authors, politicians, teachers, and church leaders tend to develop their faith from something other than the Bible. For example, the author of one "Christian" book I recently read tried to use the Bible to justify a theology that he had apparently created without any assistance at all from Scripture. Another author used his political views to shape his belief system. Too often people shape their dogmas using sources other than the Bible and then try to use its verses to validate their belief system. The simple truth is: <u>The Holy Bible</u> should be our one and only theological guide. Scripture should also be our guide to life, shaping our politics, our viewpoints, our attitudes, our lifestyle, and most of all our faith.

A myth is by definition "an invented story, idea or concept" and also "an unproved or false collective belief that is used to justify a social institution" according to Dictionary.com. For purposes of this book, the term "myth" will represent a doctrine taught as if the Bible is its origin. I will use a different myth as the title of each chapter and then explore whether the Bible supports the supposition being offered. Sometimes myths are created to soften the blow of a hard truth, to offer hope or comfort, or even to provoke fear to change behavior. May we avoid myths and cling to the words of our glorious Heavenly Father who admonishes us to learn and believe His wonderful words of life. Let's dig in.

Richard Hendrix

CHAPTER 1

EVERY PERSON IS BORN WITH A SOUL THAT WILL LIVE SOMEWHERE FOREVER

About two weeks ago, for the "millionth" time in my life, a relative reminded me that "every person is born with a soul that lives somewhere forever." If you have attended church more than a handful of times in your life you have likely heard a preacher make this same comment. This phrase, or other statements such as our "immortal soul" or our "eternal soul", has been bandied about as the truth of Scripture for as long as I have been alive and for much longer. Most who parrot these declarations say that every human being is made up of a body and soul. The body will die (if Jesus tarries) and returns to dust but the soul will immediately be transported to heaven or hell at the moment of death. The soul is the person's very essence; at its core who he really is. Some even speak of a man being a soul instead of a man having a soul. A few add spirit to the list and say that we are body, soul, and spirit usually making the latter two interchangeable terms. The body is temporary but the soul/spirit exists forever. But what does the Bible say about this concept?

The term soul in the Old Testament is the Hebrew word "nephesh". In Genesis 2:7 the Scripture says: "then the Lord God formed the man of dust from the ground and breathed into his nostrils the breath of life, and the man became a living creature (nephesh)". The KJV says in the same verse: "and man became a living soul (nephesh)." Chapter 2 continues with verse 19(b): "And whatever the man called every living creature (nephesh), that was its name." Both man and beast were called by the Bible a living nephesh, a living soul.

So do all humans and animals have souls that live somewhere forever? Let's begin at the beginning to answer that question. Look again at verse 7. God created and formed a man from the dust of the ground, specifically his body. Then He breathed into that body's nostrils the breath of life "and man became a living soul". He made the body of dust come alive with His divine breath. The body did not have a soul implanted into it; instead, God created a whole creature (nephesh) from the dust and breathed into it life.

The soul then is life to the body (i.e. its vitality and vigor). Look throughout the Old Testament and find that nephesh will represent a living, breathing body not an eternal soul. In fact, there is not one Bible verse that says the soul lives independently from the body in any situation much less in a condition of bliss in heaven or torment in hell. The soul can seek for God (Psalm 42:1); be sad and grieved (Genesis 42:21), weep and languish (Deuteronomy 28:65), rejoice (Psalm 35:9), bless the Lord (Psalm 103:1), be distressed (Job 30:25), be anxious and troubled (Psalm 6:3), and deeply love (1 Samuel 18:1). The soul can die. The prophet Ezekiel tells us twice, once in 18:4 and, for emphasis, in 18:20 that "The soul who sins shall die." In other words, the Bible tells us the soul can and will run the gamut of all human emotions, needs, desires, and feelings because the soul (nephesh) is simply another word for a living, breathing creature. The soul who sins shall die because people die.

What about the New Testament rendering of soul? The Greek word for soul is "psuche" and carries essentially the same meaning as the Hebrew word nephesh. The soul refers to a living person. For example, in Matthew 2:19-20: "But when Herod died, behold, an angel of the Lord appeared in a dream to Joseph in Egypt, saying, "Rise, take the child and his mother and go to the land of Israel, for those who sought the child's life (psuche) are dead." Later in the same book in Chapter 20 verse 28, Jesus said: "the Son of Man came not to be served but to serve, and to give his life (psuche) as a ransom for many". In a parable Jesus said that death is the result when God requires your soul. Luke 12:20: "But God said to him, 'Fool! This night your soul (psuche) is required of you, and the things you have prepared, whose will they be?" The apostle Peter tells us that souls can be purified by the truth (1 Peter 1:22) and entrusted to God (1 Peter 4:19). They can be strengthened by ministry (Acts 14:22). The word can be singular or plural as in Acts when three thousand souls "received his word and were baptized."

However, the New Testament also states that the soul can die. Acts 27:22 says: "Yet now I urge you to take heart, for there will be no loss of life (psuche) among you, but only of the ship. Furthermore, Acts 3:22-23 has: "Moses said, 'The Lord God will raise up for you a prophet like me from your brothers. You shall listen to him in what-ever he tells you. And it shall be that every soul who does not listen to that prophet shall be destroyed from the people.'" And what about Mark 8:36: "For what shall it profit a man, if he shall gain the whole world, and lose his own soul?" (KJV) And the most telling of all are the words of Jesus in Matthew 10:28: "And do not fear those who kill the body but cannot kill the soul. Rather fear him who can destroy both soul and body in hell." The soul can obviously be destroyed.

Once again the idea of an immortal soul separated from the body after death is not presented in the New Testament either. Only one place can even remotely suggest this idea: "obtaining the outcome of your faith, the salvation of your souls." (1 Peter 1:9) And even this passage does not indicate Peter is talking to his readers about an eternal separation of the soul from the body in heaven. Instead, he is encouraging Christians in the early church to persevere during intense tribulation at the hands of Rome. He is most likely talking about the saving of their lives during difficult days.

Some theologians cite Genesis 1:26-27 as proof that every human being has an eternal soul. These verses read: "26 Then God said, 'Let us make man in our image, after our likeness. And let them have dominion over the fish of the sea and over the birds of the heavens and over the livestock and over all the earth and over every creeping thing that creeps on the earth.' 27 So God created man in his own image, in the image of God he created him; male and female he created them." The thought process is that being made in God's image means that human beings, or more directly their souls, are eternal just like God. As already proven the Bible doesn't say that anywhere in the Scripture and there is certainly not a strong inference here either. How then is a man made in the image of God? That is, how is a human being made differently from plants, animals, birds, oceans, mountains, deserts, or any other of God's creation? It is mankind's ability to think, to reason, to have emotions, and to act beyond a God-given instinct. Most important of all, a human being can create. Look around at just a few of the marvelous creations of people: skyscrapers, bridges, artificial hearts and limbs, spaceships, super computers, and items of technology that weren't even science fiction a hundred years ago. God made something unique, something special in human beings. We are different from all other forms of God's creation because we were made in His image.

So if the soul is clearly not immortal, what about the spirit? There are four key verses in the New Testament that speak of the spirit of man. (The Spirit of God is mentioned much more frequently and is always translated with a capital "S" as Spirit). The word "spirit" is the common Greek word pneuma, meaning "breathing, the breath of life."

Perhaps the most famous declaration of the word "spirit" occurred when Jesus spoke the last of His "seven last sayings on the cross". Luke 23:46 says: "Then Jesus, calling out with a loud voice, said, 'Father, into your hands I commit my spirit!' And having said this he breathed his last." Jesus died quoting Psalm 31:5 only adding the word "Father" to make the verse more intimate and complete. That verse was the prayer that every Jewish mother would have taught her children to say just before going to bed. As a devout Jew, Jesus almost certainly would have spoken these words in an evening prayer his entire life. Despite His suffering and knowing this was the Father's will, these words show a deep and abiding commitment to God. Christ vocalized His unshakeable trust in God to accomplish His will in the future. This was the climax of a life humbly submitted to God from the cradle to Golgotha. In His last breath of life, the Lord turned over the "breath of life" to His Father.

Another verse that mentions the spirit is Hebrews 4:12 which reads: "For the word of God is living and active, sharper than any two-edged sword, piercing to the division of soul and of spirit, of joints and of marrow, and discerning the thoughts and intentions of the heart". The unknown author of Hebrews is making a point about the vibrancy and importance of the word of God. The expression "soul and of spirit" should be understood in the context in which it was written. The point of the verse is not that it's possible to separate soul (psuche) from spirit (pneuma). The words, as already discussed, have similar meanings in the Greek. Instead, the point is that God's Word is alive, active and sharp.

Continue to 1 Thessalonians 5:23 where Paul writes: "Now may the God of peace himself sanctify you completely, and may your whole spirit and soul and body be kept blameless at the coming of our Lord Jesus Christ". The apostle's focus is not on differentiating soul and spirit but is attempting to quantify the whole nature of man on all sides. That is, let everything about you be sanctified (set apart) completely and be blameless at the coming of our Lord.

Finally, 1 Corinthians 15:45 reads: "Thus it is written, 'the first man Adam became a living being (soul); the last Adam became a life-giving spirit.'" The last Adam is, of course, Jesus. Paul is writing to the Corinthian church about a heresy that had developed within the fellowship that Christ did not rise from the grave. The apostle is making it clear to the believers at Corinth that Jesus did indeed have a bodily resurrection in human form and then ascended to heaven with the Father.

In Ecclesiastes 12:7 the Preacher (most commonly thought to be Solomon) finished his book advising young people to remember God before: "the dust returns to the earth as it was, and the spirit returns to God who gave it." The spirit once again is the breath of life as Solomon encourages his readers to cherish God before they die. Other Old Testament verses such as Numbers 16:22 and 27:16 carry forward the same theme.

So according to Scripture the soul represents life; a living, breathing creature. The spirit is the breath of life provided by our Creator. The Bible does not say that the soul or spirit will live on forever separated from the body. Instead, the Word of God indicates plainly that the "soul that sins will die." If Jesus tarries, every living soul (person and animal) will die and their spirit (breath of life) will pass from them. The soul is not eternal and neither is our spirit for "it is appointed for man to die once, and after that comes judgment. (Hebrews 9:27)". But the wonderful news is that God can be trusted with our spirit until Christ returns. As believers we can pray with Christ that if we die today "Father, into your hands we commit our spirit". We need not fear that death is the end for our Savior promises that we will live again when He returns for His church. The Gospel in miniature, John 3:16, says: "For God so loved the world, that he gave his only Son, that whoever believes in him should not perish but have eternal life." God will restore the breath of life to those who knew Him. And this time it will be forever.

CHAPTER 2

REPENTANCE THAT LEADS TO SALVATION IS A TURNING AWAY FROM SIN

REPENT OR BURN IN HELL!!!!! Or at least that's what the sign said that was next to the highway near my house. About two trees to the right another large sign read "DON'T LOSE YOUR SOUL BY THE MARK OF THE BEAST, JESUS CAN SAVE US". The signs were posted on private property and for years warned passersby that they had better repent and avoid the mark of the beast or certain destruction would follow. I remember those predictions were posted there from the time I learned to read until I was at least high school age. Many eyes saw the message on those two signs through the years.

Since my family didn't attend church of any kind on a regular basis, most of the theology I learned as a child came from such places as road signs, friends at school, and the occasional radio broadcast. Now as any inquisitive youngster would do, especially one who didn't want to burn in hell, I began to ask questions about the meaning of these sayings. Unfortunately, the more people I asked, the more varied and wildly dissimilar were the responses. I'm convinced that even today someone inquiring about the meaning of "REPENT OR BURN IN HELL" would probably be offered a rather diverse set of rejoinders.

The word repent, as used in Scripture, has been discussed in religious circles for years with various meanings propagated by those who believed they understood why God put this word in His book. Most theologians have made repentance a test of faith, that is, without repentance there is no salvation. But that doesn't answer the question: what is repentance that leads to salvation? Something so important that my faith (and ultimately my relationship with God) depends on it must be defined. Some say it is to be remorseful, conscious stricken, and sorry about your sin. Others say it means changing your ways. You are so regretful of your past actions that you modify your behavior to avoid those actions. Still others say that to repent means to turn away from your sin, ask forgiveness, and perform penitence often before a priest. I have even heard it said that once you recognize how appalling your sin is to God, that you see sin as God sees it, you will then stop sinning. This is true repentance. Are any of these in line with the Bible?

Let's look at Biblical references to repentance and see if we can get a clear understanding of this important word. A few examples in the Old Testament are:

a) Nineveh in the Book of Jonah. These wicked people heard the word of the prophet, repented and God spared their city. Jonah 3:5 reads: "And the people of Nineveh believed God. They called for a fast and put on sackcloth, from the greatest of them to the least of them." Putting on sackcloth was a symbol of remorse and sorrow for their sin.

b) In Job chapter 42, Job answers God by saying "therefore I despise myself, and repent in dust and ashes." Repent here means "to take comfort" in the surroundings. The ESV says the Hebrew word for repent used here means "am comforted".

c) 1 Kings 8:48: "if they repent with all their mind and with all their heart in the land of their enemies, who carried them captive, and pray to you toward their land"...8:49: "then hear in heaven your dwelling place their prayer and their plea, and maintain their cause". The Hebrew people are pleading their case to God because of a change of mind and heart.

d) Another, Ezekiel 14:6: "Therefore say to the house of Israel, Thus says the Lord God: Repent and turn away from your idols, and turn away your faces from all your abominations."

Some form of the word repent appears 46 times in the KJV Old Testament. None of these phrases are related to our salvation experience. In 28 of the 46 occurrences the Bible says God repented of a certain action. For example, Exodus 32:14 in the KJV: "And the Lord repented of the evil which he thought to do unto his people." God cannot sin so He did not have to turn from any wrongdoing or have remorse or change His mind. Instead, God relented (see ESV). The Lord made an agreement with Abraham "I will multiply your offspring as the stars of heaven, and all this land that I have promised I will give to your offspring, and they shall inherit it forever." To keep that promise our Sovereign God did not bring His wrath upon Israel. When the Old Testament mentions a man or a nation repenting it involves one of these results:

a) A sign of remorse and sorrow as in Ninevah

b) A place of comfort in surroundings as in Job

c) changing mind and heart as in 1 Kings

d) turning away from idols and from all abominations as in Ezekiel

e) relenting as God did to keep His promises

Again, none of the instances of repentance in the Old Testament has anything to do with a person's eternal destiny.

Here are more from the New Testament:

a) Mark 1:14-15 reads "Now after John was arrested, Jesus came into Galilee, proclaiming the gospel of God, and saying, 'The time is fulfilled, and the kingdom of God is at hand; repent and believe in the gospel.'"

b) In Luke 13:3 these words of Jesus are recorded: "No, I tell you; but unless you repent, you will all likewise perish."

c) In Acts 20:21 Paul was speaking to the Ephesian elders about his ministry since he had arrived in Asia, where he had been: "testifying both to Jews and to Greeks of repentance toward God and of faith in our Lord Jesus Christ." Later in chapter 26 during his defense before Festus, Paul remarked in verse 20: "but declared first to those in Damascus, then in Jerusalem and throughout all the region of Judea, and also to the Gentiles, that they should repent and turn to God, performing deeds in keeping with their repentance."

d) In Revelation 2:5 John renders the words of the Lord to the first century church at Ephesus: "Remember therefore from where you have fallen; repent, and do the works you did at first. If not, I will come to you and remove your lampstand from its place, unless you repent."

John the Baptist preached a message of repentance. So did Paul, John, and Christ Himself. Clearly, repentance is an important doctrinal truth and, as we've seen, the word carries different meanings in Scripture. But Jesus said "unless you repent, you will all likewise perish". There is a repentance that leads to salvation. What is the meaning of that word?

When I was a teenager and in early manhood I recall that the definition of repentance that leads to faith was to be sorry or broken over our sin. Many messages were presented that true repentance meant to be so grieved, so mournful over our sin that we become contrite and change our ways. Paul tells us in 2 Corinthians 7:10: "For godly grief produces a repentance that leads to salvation without regret, whereas worldly grief produces death." Godly grief may produce repentance but grief, in and of itself, is not the same as repentance. I have heard many preachers and teachers talk about the grief and sorrow they felt over their sin before they were saved. What is the implication? That we must be sorrowful and broken before we can come to God? How sorrowful? How broken? Christ's finished work has delivered our salvation. No amount of remorse will buy the favor of God or help us present our case to the Savior.

The definition of repentance that leads to salvation changed slightly as I grew older. I remember vividly one Sunday at church when our Minister of Education spoke about repentance as a turning away from our sin. He used the example of walking with sin by walking across the platform away from the pulpit and then, abruptly, he turned 180° and began walking in the opposite direction. According to this minister "the original language means turning away from our sin and going the other direction." He went on to say that "to be saved, a person must repent; that is, turn away from your sin." I used this example several times when teaching my own Bible study classes. Apparently many others believed the same way because I saw that analogy over and over. The general idea was: "stop sinning, have faith and God will give you a new heart." However, there is a fatal flaw with that teaching. In this life, none of us are capable of turning away and leaving our sin behind. If turning from our sin means to stop sinning everyone has missed the mark and nobody can be saved. The apostle John wrote in 1 John 1:10: "If we say we have not sinned, we make him (God) a liar, and his word is not in us." Paul confirms this in

Romans 3:23: "for all have sinned and fall short of the glory of God" right after he said in verse 10 of the same chapter: "None is righteous, no, not one." Besides all that, if our relationship with God depends on our ability to walk away from sin, why did Jesus have to come and die on the cross?

Repentance is not a character overhaul. To repent does not mean to reform behavior, restore broken relationships, or commit to a church or some good cause. Many in the Christian faith have adapted the philosophy of most world religions by claiming that a person must do "something" to earn a relationship with God. The "something" might mean joining a particular church, being baptized in a certain way, doing penance, living a certain lifestyle, or numerous other functions that earn our position with the Father. The Bible's teaching about salvation is both profound and mysterious. Salvation is a gift and there is nothing any of us can do to earn it. Over and over Scripture reminds us that God is the author of redemption. God provided it at a great cost to Him but free to us. Consider these verses:

John 1:12 – "But to all who did receive him, who believed in his name, he gave the right to become children of God."

Ephesians 2:8-9 – "For by grace you have been saved through faith. And this is not your own doing; it is the gift of God, not a result of works, so that no one may boast."

Titus 3:5 – "he (God) saved us, not because of works done by us in righteousness, but according to his own mercy, by the washing of regeneration and renewal of the Holy Spirit."

Romans 6:23 – "For the wages of sin is death, but the free gift of God is eternal life in Christ Jesus our Lord"

This is but a small sample of the verses that remind us salvation is free. And yet, many people cannot accept this fact and offer up ways for human beings to have a part in God's deliverance. Most often this is done under the guise of repentance. The precept is that repentance involves "something" that we must do to earn God's favor.

Some theologians get the cart before the horse. The teaching is that we turn from our sin, believe, and we are saved. In contrast, the Bible teaches that we repent, believe and are saved and then we allow the Holy Spirit to deal with the sins in our lives.

Obviously repentance that leads to salvation does not mean being sorrowful and broken nor is it a turning away from sin because not one person lives a life (or likely even a day) without sin. These teachings are damaging because many people reject Christ because they cannot live up to the moral standard that either a) I'm not broken-hearted enough or b) that a true Christian will have no sin. Furthermore, repentance is not living a reformed life that somehow causes God to love us more than when we were in our unregenerate (unrepentant) state. While I've heard dozens of sermons end with an invitation that starts with "Repent of your sins and" that phrase is certainly not commanded, or even mentioned, anywhere in Scripture.

Considering all of this as what "repentance that leads to salvation" is not, let's look deeper at what it really is. The word repent, in one form or another, is found in the New Testament over 60 times. The Greek words metanoia a noun of the verb metanoeo are the two words used by Jesus, John the Baptist and others to reflect an action required on our part. The Greek Dictionary indicates these words have the same meaning: "to change one's mind." To believe in Jesus, a person must "change one's mind" about his fitness for heaven and put his faith in Christ as the only way to be saved. The action required on our part always occurs when we encounter the true and living God. Here are a few examples:

- In Isaiah Chapter 6 when the prophet had a vision of being in the presence of God. Isaiah's response to being before God: "5 And I said: 'Woe is me! For I am lost; for I am a man of unclean lips, and I dwell in the midst of a people of unclean lips; for my eyes have seen the King, the Lord of hosts!' 6 Then one of the seraphim flew to me, having in his hand a burning coal that he had taken with tongs from the altar. 7 And he touched my mouth and said: 'Behold, this has touched your lips; your guilt is taken away, and your sin atoned for.'"

- At the transfiguration of our Lord described in Matthew Chapter 17, Peter, James and John literally heard the voice of God and "6 When the disciples heard this, they fell on their faces and were terrified."

- Dr. Luke described a fishing expedition when Jesus miraculously filled a large boat with fish to the point that it was about to sink. Peter had fished all night and had taken nothing but at the Lord's command the disciples caught so many fish the ship began to sink. "8 But when Simon Peter saw it, he fell down at Jesus' knees, saying, "Depart from me, for I am a sinful man, O Lord."

- In the Book of Revelation Chapter 1 John writes of seeing the risen savior in person. How does John respond? "17 When I saw him, I fell at his feet as though dead. But he laid his right hand on me, saying, 'Fear not, I am the first and the last, 18 and the living one. I died, and behold I am alive forevermore, and I have the keys of Death and Hades.'"

Do you see a trend here? Every person who truly encountered God responded in the same way. These men saw God as He really is: holy, righteous, great, and powerful. But they also recognized their own shortcomings, their sin, and weakness. They did not react to God in arrogance or in a flippant way. Instead, they recognized their own sinfulness and need for a Savior. True repentance that leads to salvation means that we are convicted of our sin and change our mind about our fitness for heaven and a relationship with God. We admit that God's grace, his unmerited favor, invites us to have a relationship with Him and not anything that we have done or ever will do is enough to gain His favor.

Jesus spoke often of the hypocrisy of the scribes and Pharisees. The Lord exposed their ridiculous assertion that because they were sons of Abraham these men had gained favor with God. The Savior taught that authority and riches have nothing to do with a relationship to The Almighty. Christ rebuked these men for clinging to their birthright and accomplishments for their salvation and the lesson is ours today. As mentioned earlier, many people believe that a person must earn favor with God by carrying out some deed or action. Somehow when we have fulfilled this righteous act—whatever it is—we find favor with God. The Lord said to repent of this thinking; that is, change your mind and put your faith and trust in Christ and in Him alone. Repentance that leads to salvation means to change your mind about your worthiness to God. Lay aside everything else and accept God's gracious gift.

In Paul's epistle to the Romans in Chapter 2, the apostle warned those who judge others but ignore their own wrongdoing in verse 3: "Do you suppose, O man—you who judge those who practice such things and yet do them yourself—that you will escape the judgment of God?" Paul was focusing on people who believed they had favor with God because they were Jews who read and understood the law. Paul went on to say in verse 13 that: "For it is not the hearers of the law who are righteous before God, but the doers of the law who will be justified." Those who knew the law had broken the law but were convinced they had favor with God despite doing the same things as the men they condemned. In Acts 17:30 Paul summed up the solution: "The times of ignorance God overlooked, but now he commands all people everywhere to repent". Change your mind about what you have done to earn salvation and accept God's glorious and free gift of salvation. Isaiah 64:6 says in the KJV: "But we are all as an unclean thing, and all our righteousnesses are as filthy rags". The very best we can bring to God is as filthy rags in his sight. We don't measure up no matter how well we think we live.

How then do we have a relationship with a Holy God when we recognize we are sinners and cannot save ourselves? How do we accept the free gift God is offering? How do we repent and believe so that we do not perish? Look at these passages:

John 3:16 – "For God so loved the world, that he gave his only Son, that whoever believes in him should not perish but have eternal life."

John 3:36 – "Whoever believes in the Son has eternal life;"

John 20:31 – "But these are written, that ye might believe that Jesus is the Christ, the Son of God; and that believing ye might have life through his name."

Acts 16:29-31 is the story of Paul with the Philippian jailer. Paul and Silas had been beaten and thrown into prison. A great earthquake occurred and the stocks fell off all of the prisoners. The jailer was about to kill himself when Paul told him: "Do not harm yourself, for we are all here." Listen to what happened next: "29 And the jailer called for lights and rushed in, and trembling with fear he fell down before Paul and Silas. 30 Then he brought them out and said, 'Sirs, what must I do to be saved?' 31 And they said, 'Believe in the Lord Jesus, and you will be saved, you and your household.'"

The answer is to repent and believe. Accept without question your unworthiness for heaven. Instead put your faith and trust in Jesus Christ and His finished work. By removing ourselves from the equation by changing our minds about our worth to God and say as the Lord said from the cross: "Father, into your hands, we commit our spirit." Believing is more than just an assent that Jesus came, died, and rose again. To truly believe means to place our eternal future into the magnificence of this truth. Repent, that is, change your mind about trusting anything you have ever done that will earn everlasting life. This is the true repentance that leads to salvation.

CHAPTER 3

THE STORY OF THE RICH MAN AND LAZARUS DESCRIBES THE AFTERLIFE

When searching Scripture for truth it is imperative to read Bible passages in context. On a broad scale this means reading the entire Word of God instead of selecting individual verses or just a few passages to develop a doctrine or belief system. I will talk about this in greater detail later in the book. But as we research individual topics it is important to look at the background and setting of the message being presented. Why is this important? Without understanding the context of what is presented the meaning may be distorted and we may miss the nugget God has for us. That is why it is important to understand the parables of Luke 16 one must go back to the previous chapter to set the stage.

Luke Chapter 15 begins with this declaration: "Now the tax collectors and sinners were all drawing near to hear him (Jesus). And the Pharisees and the scribes grumbled, saying, 'This man receives sinners and eats with them.'" The context is this: Jesus is speaking to His disciples and to certain "sinners" who came to hear Him. The Lord launches into a series of parables. His enemies are listening closely and comment derisively after several of the parables. Jesus followed the parables of the lost sheep, the lost coin, and the lost son with two very strong indictments against the Pharisees and teachers of the law: The Parable of the Dishonest Manager and The Rich Man and Lazarus.

Here is the former, often called The Parable of the Unjust Steward, from Luke 16:1-9:

"He also said to the disciples, There was a rich man who had a manager, and charges were brought to him that this man was wasting his possessions. And he called him and said to him, 'What is this that I hear about you? Turn in the account of your management, for you can no longer be manager.' And the manager said to himself, 'What shall I do, since my master is taking the management away from me? I am not strong enough to dig, and I am ashamed to beg. I have decided what to do, so that when I am removed from management, people may receive me into their houses.' So, summoning his master's debtors one by one, he said to the first, 'How much do you owe my master?' He said, 'A hundred measures of oil.' He said to him, 'Take your bill, and sit down quickly and write fifty.' Then he said to another, 'And how much do you owe?' He said, 'A hundred measures of wheat.' He said to him, 'Take your bill, and write eighty.' The master commended the dishonest manager for his shrewdness. For the sons of this world are more shrewd in dealing with their own generation than the sons of light. And I tell you, make friends for yourselves by means of unrighteous wealth, so that when it fails they may receive you into the eternal dwellings."

Here is my paraphrase of the story using today's business environment. An employer finds that one of his managers has been wasting company assets. He calls in the manager, demands an accounting of his dealings, and sets in motions plans to discharge him. The dishonest steward both unwilling to work or to beg develops a scheme in which he goes to the employer's customers and strikes a bargain with them to pay less than what they actually owe. By working these debtors in this way, he believes that they will support him after he leaves the employer. The employer learns of the scheme and calls in the former manager but instead of having him arrested the employer commends the man for his shrewdness.

You can count on one hand the number of times I have heard this passage preached over my lifetime. The few times that I have were almost comical as teachers try to get from "make friends for yourselves by means of unrighteous wealth" to verse 13 of the same chapter: "No servant can serve two masters, for either he will hate the one and love the other, or he will be devoted to the one and despise the other. You cannot serve God and money." Some explain this parable as Jesus commending the shrewdness of the manager but not his dishonesty. They claim that Jesus is bragging on the manager's cleverness and foresight as he chooses a sensible way to solve his problem. They then claim that "unrighteous wealth" is a euphemism for money and that the lesson in this parable is that Christians should use their "unrighteous wealth" (a.k.a. money) to do well in this world. We should as Christians be more like the world—that is shrewd—in the way we handle money. Others say Jesus is condemning the manager's actions but that the master in the parable recognized the shrewdness of his manager and being of a like mind commended the man for what he had done. That is the master is in essence saying "I would have done the same thing were I in your shoes." These commentators say the lesson is that Jesus taught that Christians should be diametrically opposed to the methods of the unjust steward and his master. As an alternative to the steward and master Jesus is saying to his followers to be faithful in the way they handle money. The steward and the master were both treacherous but Christians should be the opposite.

These explanations are so far-fetched that a reasonable person must quickly and emphatically reject them. No employer in his right mind would ever commend his manager for unscrupulous actions as these. Likewise Jesus would never commend this manager for stealing from his master after being justifiably fired for wasting the rich man's resources. Such events never happened and never will happen.

Instead, the Lord is telling a story of the preposterous position being lived out by the Pharisees and scribes. The Jewish leaders controlled the wealth of the temple but they used their position to gain wealth for themselves. God told Abraham in Genesis 12:2: "And I will make of you a great nation, and I will bless you and make your name great, so that you will be a blessing." The Jewish people were set aside by God from the time of Abraham to be a blessing to the world. It is through Israel that God determined to bring the Jewish Messiah and our Savior and Lord into the world. But these scribes and Pharisees hated non-Jews and instead of being a blessing to the world they were corrupt, ignored the teachings of God and lived to perpetuate their own importance and power. They looked upon themselves with pride and arrogance. They believed because the people honored and praised them that they had somehow obtained God's favor. But the Messiah's words told a different story. These men had wasted the blessings of God and Jesus brought them to account for this. These men and their ancestors had murdered the messengers of God and now were about to do the same to the very Son of God.

The Lord concluded the parable with this outrageous statement: "And I tell you, make friends for yourselves by means of unrighteous wealth, so that when it fails they may receive you into the eternal dwellings." The statement is dripping with irony. In essence Christ said this: "live life chasing after unrighteous wealth, so that when your efforts fail God will welcome you into heaven." Christ is saying that these men truly believed they could spend their lives cheating the masses, ignoring God's law, and living a corrupt existence but expecting to be provided eternal life and luxury when they died. Why? Because they were descendants of Abraham and were God's chosen people. This parable is a strong rebuke of these men and their hypocritical and misguided values. Much as the unjust manager cheated his master but expected reward, so the Pharisees and scribes expected eternal favor from God. Jesus showed the absurdity of their thinking in this parable. Sad to say but don't most people in the world today think they can reject God in this life but be rewarded with eternal paradise when they die?

But our Savior wasn't finished condemning the scribes and Pharisees. After a short discourse on divorce, He went on to further denounce the Jewish leaders. One of the most controversial passages in the entire Bible is the story of the rich man and Lazarus appearing in Luke 16:19-31. I called the passage a "story" because there is a great deal of contention as to whether the details are history or a parable. Some argue that the events described in these verses actually occurred and Jesus is describing the outcome; others say that it is a parable used to teach a lesson to the listeners. The Lord often used parables to teach some truth, principle, or moral lesson.

Here are the verses Luke 16 that tell this story in the more familiar King James Version:

19 There was a certain rich man, which was clothed in purple and fine linen, and fared sumptuously every day:20 And there was a certain beggar named Lazarus, which was laid at his gate, full of sores,21 And desiring to be fed with the crumbs which fell from the rich man's table: moreover the dogs came and licked his sores.22 And it came to pass, that the beggar died, and was carried by the angels into Abraham's bosom: the rich man also died, and was buried;23 And in hell he lifted up his eyes, being in torments, and seeth Abraham afar off, and Lazarus in his bosom.24 And he cried and said, Father Abraham, have mercy on me, and send Lazarus, that he may dip the tip of his finger in water, and cool my tongue; for I am tormented in this flame.25 But Abraham said, Son, remember that thou in thy lifetime receivedst thy good things, and likewise Lazarus evil things: but now he is comforted, and thou art tormented.26 And beside all this, between us and you there is a great gulf fixed: so that

they which would pass from hence to you cannot; neither can they pass to us, that would come from thence.27 Then he said, I pray thee therefore, father, that thou wouldest send him to my father's house:28 For I have five brethren; that he may testify unto them, lest they also come into this place of torment.29 Abraham saith unto him, They have Moses and the prophets; let them hear them.30 And he said, Nay, father Abraham: but if one went unto them from the dead, they will repent.31 And he said unto him, If they hear not Moses and the prophets, neither will they be persuaded, though one rose from the dead.

Is this history or a parable? Note the first statement, "There was a certain rich man". Jesus most often started his parables with the phrases "certain man", "certain rich man", and "certain nobleman". In fact, eight times in the Book of Luke alone, Jesus began a parable with one of those phrases. It is logical that Jesus is beginning another parable. Next, notice that Jesus neither accuses the rich man of any unrighteousness nor does he portray Lazarus as a believer. The rich man simply lived a life of wealth receiving good things while Lazarus had the misfortune of being sick (the dogs licked his sores) and so poor he had to beg to survive. If the story is history, rich people are destined for hell while homeless folk who beg are all going to heaven. Third, no person can enter the bosom defined as the chest or breast of another human being. This is a physical impossibility. Clearly there is figurative language involved to describe Lazarus inside Abraham's bosom. Fourth, if this is a literal story, then saved people will be able to see those who are in hell and vice versa. Imagine spending eternity watching friends and loved ones suffer excruciating pain in fire and brimstone. Fifth, a man burning in fire and brimstone would not request just one drop of water to relieve the pain and suffering. What about the rest of his body? Finally, Jesus describes the rich man as having a body in hell with eyes, mouth, and tongue. This has to be symbolic language because both science and theology agree the body dies and the remains of the rich man's body would be buried and returned to dust. So, without question, unless all of the points of the story are factual then we must see the story as a parable given to the listeners to teach a spiritual truth. Let's investigate further.

The parable begins with the statement about the rich man being clothed in purple and fine linen. The wearing of purple always represented wealth and sometimes royalty. But the next description, fine linen, was specific for the priesthood. Exodus 28:39 describes the priestly garment: "You shall weave the coat in checker work of fine linen, and you shall make a turban of fine linen, and you shall make a sash embroidered with needlework." The Lord is referring to a priest when He says the rich man is clothed in fine linen. God refers to Israel as "a kingdom of priests and a holy nation." It is reasonable then to see that the rich man in this parable represents Israel. God, for reasons of His own, chose Israel as his special people from the foundation of the world. The Jews were indeed rich. Rich in God's presence, blessings, and protection these people continued in a cycle of sin and rededication throughout the Old Testament. They tended to be self-righteous glorifying the gifts God gave them instead of the Holy provider of the gifts. As mentioned earlier, instead of being a blessing to all nations, they became the enemy of their neighbors and spent many years in captivity to those they hated. At this point in history only the Jews had the knowledge of the one true God. Truly the nation would be cast as wearing purple and fine linen because they were rich beyond measure and a "kingdom of priests". Furthermore, Jesus went on to say the rich man was a Jew when he said about his brothers: "They have Moses and the prophets; let them hear them."

Who then is Lazarus? The first thing to note is that he is a beggar. Gentiles are easily seen as beggars. Paul wrote in Ephesians 2:12 to Gentile believers: "remember that you were at that time separated from Christ, alienated from the commonwealth of Israel and strangers to the covenants of promise, having no hope and without God in the world." At the time Christ spoke this parable, Gentiles were "alien-ated from Israel" and hated by the Jews as second class citizens or worse. Non-Jews "had no knowledge of the covenants of promise" that is, no Scripture or any knowledge of God. They had "no hope" and were "without God in the world". Gentiles were forced to beg for spiritual crumbs from God's favored people. Jesus goes on to say that dogs came to comfort Lazarus and licked his sores. The beggar, already perceived as unclean, was attended to by unclean animals. The imagery is of the beggar being a Gentile, a dog in the eyes of these self-righteous men. Jesus Himself used this description when He met the Syrophoenician woman in Mark 7:24-30: "And he said to her, "Let the children be fed first, for it is not right to take the chil-dren's bread and throw it to the dogs." Jesus used the word "children" to represent the Jews and the word "dogs" to represent the Gentiles. Clearly Lazarus represents Gentiles.

So, what is the point of this parable? Most Jews held two popular beliefs that Jesus contradicted with this parable:

1) It was a sign of blessing from God if you were rich. If you were poor there was a curse on you from God presumably because of your sin.

2) If you were a descendant of Abraham then you were guaranteed a place in heaven.

In this parable, the rich man (the Jewish aristocrat) was burning in hell and the poor man (the Gentile) was safe in Abraham's bosom. This scenario would be unthinkable in this culture. The story is now so outrageous to the listeners that it would spark immediate outrage and visceral disagreement.

This parable has nothing to do with a literal heaven or a literal hell. It is a rebuke to the Jews who believed that because of their ancestry they had an open-door invitation to heaven. Jewish leaders of that day were commonly divided into two groups: Sadducees and Pharisees. The Sadducees, the larger of the two groups, did not believe in a bodily resurrection and taught their followers that when all people died the body went to Sheol, a place of silence. The Pharisees, on the other hand, believed that Jews only would be resurrected from Sheol and would be carried to the bosom of Abraham, Isaac, and Jacob where they would be received and praised by their forefathers. Jesus used this common Hebrew term "bosom of Abraham" to represent the place where Lazarus was carried. See the Hebrew Bible 4 Maccabees 13:17 as an example of the teaching of this concept. Jesus used this phrase to represent a place of peace and rest where Lazarus was "carried by angels" when he died. Some scholars propose that Jesus preserved a Jewish legend when he told this parable. The point is: Lazarus was not taken to paradise or heaven in the literal sense. Instead, Jesus used a place of legend, the bosom of Abraham, to show that a poor beggar could be carried away by angels but not a rich Jewish aristocrat.

Likewise the picture of the rich man being in fiery torment is not a picture of hell. Instead it is a shocking testimony to the Pharisees and rulers of the law that God will bring judgment against all who sin, including rich Jewish men who may also happen to be priests. Hiding behind the cloak of heritage, the enemies of Jesus were exposed by this parable. The rich man died, was buried, and in hell (Sheol or Hades) he lifted up his eyes. The name can mean "dark place" or "unseen" in the Hebrew and was meant to represent a place where the dead would not be seen because they were out of favor with God. Again, Christ's listeners would have been astonished and angry at these revelations. Nothing would have upset the Lord's enemies more than this.

So here is a parable that would have shaken the Jewish leaders at their very foundation. A beggar, a Gentile, was taken up to Abraham's bosom while the rich Jewish priest was buried in Hades. The strong implication is that Israel and Gentiles were exchanging places. The Jews were being forsaken by God and Gentiles were becoming the seed of Abraham. There is a great gulf between the Jews and Abraham. Paul told the world in Romans 11:7-8 what this gulf represents: "What then? Israel failed to obtain what it was seeking. The elect obtained it, but the rest were hardened, as it is written, 'God gave them a spirit of stupor, eyes that would not see and ears that would not hear, down to this very day.'" God in His sovereignty brought salvation to the Gentiles and ordained that many Jews would be unable to recognize what God established in Christ.

In summary, this parable has nothing to do with a literal heaven or hell. It is our Lord's great teaching that salvation had come to Gentiles and that being a descendant of Abraham did not guarantee favor with God. Jesus used these two parables in Luke 16 to confound and anger his listeners while, at the same time, teaching a powerful truth we can cling to even today. All may be saved, whether Jew or Gentile, by placing faith in Jesus Christ.

CHAPTER 4

THE MOMENT AFTER MY DEATH, I'LL BE WALKING STREETS OF GOLD

Most people my age who are comfortably in their 60's have had the unfortunate duty of attending many funerals and memorial services during their lifetimes. This is certainly my experience as well. With very few exceptions the death of a relative or a friend triggered an observance that usually included a eulogy, a sermon, and music and occasionally offered poems, funny stories, and anecdotes about the deceased. Some ceremonies were long and laborious, a few were heartbreaking with weeping and shouting, others were short and solemn, and still others were filled with laughter, jokes, and good humor all around that celebrated the life of the person who had passed. Most were held in a church though some were conducted at the funeral home. A couple of times the memorial service was held in a very public place, a beach where ashes were scattered into the ocean. A clergyman almost always led the proceedings but not always. (I have presided at two funerals but am not ordained to the ministry).

But with all of the differences in the manner in which the ceremony was conducted, one general theme was true in virtually every circumstance. It was said that the person who had died was now in heaven with Jesus. The deceased was alive again, had passed through the pearly gates and now walking on streets of gold. What great comfort these comments were for those of us who had just lost a family member or a close friend. Our loved one was no longer suffering and was now shrouded in eternal joy never again forced to face trials and troubles on this planet. Oh what a joy to know that even as the words are being spoken by the person presiding, there is a great celebration taking place in heaven with grand reunions and a personal welcome from our Savior. Where in the Bible are all of these wonderful promises?

Surprisingly there are no direct references in the Scripture with these promises and only a few verses that even imply that what is being preached has any validity. I would have thought that such wonderful truth would have been stated over and over in plain language that even a child could understand. As I have listened carefully to messages about death through the years a recurring theme of text is used to convince the listener that his/her loved one is in the arms of Jesus even now.

First, in 2 Corinthians 5:8 the apostle Paul writes: "Yes, we are of good courage, and we would rather be away from the body and at home with the Lord." The same verse in the KJV: "We are confident, I say, and willing rather to be absent from the body, and to be present with the Lord." This verse is, by far, the text most often quoted at funerals except it is almost always abbreviated as "absent from the body is to be present with the Lord". In Philippians 1:21-23 Paul utters: "For to me to live is Christ, and to die is gain. If I am to live in the flesh, that means fruitful labor for me. Yet which I shall choose I cannot tell. I am hard pressed between the two. My desire is to depart and be with Christ, for that is far better." Paul, in both of these passages, is talking about transitioning from this sinful, corruptible body to being "present with the Lord".

But when does this take place?

Look in the First Corinthians Chapter 15:51-55 for one example:

Behold! I tell you a mystery. We shall not all sleep, but we shall all be changed, in a moment, in the twinkling of an eye, at the last trumpet. For the trumpet will sound, and the dead will be raised imperishable, and we shall be changed. For this perishable body must put on the imperishable, and this mortal body must put on immortality. When the perishable puts on the imperishable, and the mortal puts on immortality, then shall come to pass the saying that is written: "Death is swallowed up in victory." "O death, where is your victory? O death, where is your sting?"

When did Paul say this perishable puts on the imperishable in this passage? He clarifies in this response when we will be present with the Lord. The clear answer is: at the last trumpet when Christ returns for His people the dead will be raised imperishable. Wouldn't this have been the perfect place for Paul to say that the perishable puts on the imperishable immediately when we die? But he did not.

How about another example? First Thessalonians 4:16-17 Paul writes: "For the Lord himself will descend from heaven with a cry of command, with the voice of an archangel, and with the sound of the trumpet of God. And the dead in Christ will rise first. Then we who are alive, who are left, will be caught up together with them in the clouds to meet the Lord in the air, and so we will always be with the Lord." Again the same answer, the dead will rise together when Christ returns for His church at his second coming.

Finally, here's a third clear passage Paul gave us to make sure we understand when we will be with the Lord: 1 Corinthians 15:20-23: "But in fact Christ has been raised from the dead, the firstfruits of those who have fallen asleep. For as by a man came death, by a man has come also the resurrection of the dead. For as in Adam all die, so also in Christ shall all be made alive. But each in his own order: Christ the firstfruits, then at his coming those who belong to Christ." All men die but Jesus will make all alive. When will this happen? Verse 23 is clear: "Christ the firstfruits, then at his coming those who belong to

Christ." Passage after passage Paul makes clear that believers will be alive again when (and only when) Christ returns.

Paul has clarified over and over when he would be with Christ. There is nothing in these verses that remotely indicate that the moment he died, he expected to be in the presence of Christ. He simply states the simple truth of all believers, that to be with Christ will be far better than to be laboring on this earth. Paul was beaten, stoned, betrayed, and imprisoned for most of the latter years of his life. No wonder he wanted to depart this life to be with Christ. However, Paul does not say: "the moment I die I will be absent from this body and present with the Lord." Nor does he write anywhere in Scripture that the instant a person dies, the soul is carried into heaven. Paul wrote much of the New Testament but never said one time that simple statement that would mean so much to us as believers—our loved ones at death immediately go to be with Jesus. If this were the case he would have trumpeted this glorious truth over and over. Let me repeat for emphasis, Paul never says anywhere that believers who die immediately go to heaven to be with Christ.

Paul comments further on this subject when he speaks of the believers' citizenship in heaven. In Philippians Chapter 3:20-21 he writes: "But our citizenship is in heaven, and from it we await a Savior, the Lord Jesus Christ, who will transform our lowly body to be like his glorious body, by the power that enables him even to subject all things to himself." What did Paul say? We are not citizens of this world waiting for our journey to heaven. Instead, we are already citizens of heaven as we live out our lives here until all things become new. For what are we waiting? Not death, but for "a Savior, the Lord Jesus Christ, who will transform our lowly body to be like his glorious body." We will see Christ when He returns.

Sometimes to convince listeners that a deceased love one is now home in heaven a preacher will quote Jesus speaking to the thief on the cross. Almost every time the phrase is "Jesus said: Today you will be with me in paradise." The logical conclusion is that if the thief was in paradise with Jesus that day then believers who have died since then will experience the same fate. Here is the entire conversation from Luke Chapter 23, verses 42 and 43: "And he said, "Jesus, remember me when you come into your kingdom." And he said to him, "Truly, I say to you, today you will be with me in Paradise." Notice what the thief was asking, "Jesus, remember me when you come into your kingdom." Jesus had spoken about God's kingdom or the kingdom of heaven dozens of times during his ministry. The kingdom of heaven is represented as the second coming of our Lord, the time He returns to this earth, judges his enemies, and establishes His kingdom here. The Savior taught His followers to pray: "thy kingdom come", clearly a future event when "thy will be done on earth as it is in heaven." The thief is asking to be remembered when Christ comes into His kingdom, at His second coming. The confusion about the response of our Lord is because of the man-made addition of a comma. Move the comma one word to the right and Jesus answered: "Truly, I say to you today, you will be with me in Paradise." How can we be sure this is the meaning? He certainly had not established His kingdom on this earth on that day and, as of this writing, has not done so yet. Most importantly, Jesus didn't go to paradise that day; He was dead and in the grave. Christ was raised from the dead by God on the third day. This is the most fundamental teaching of Christianity. The apostle Paul even said: "And if Christ has not been raised, then our preaching is in vain and your faith is in vain. We are even found to be misrepresenting God, because we testified about God that he raised Christ" in 1 Corinthians 15:14-15. He continues in verse 19 that if Christ didn't die, be buried, and be resurrected on the third day, "we are of all people most to be pitied". There is no Biblical evidence that Jesus did anything except what He said He would do in Matthew 17:22-23: "As they were gathering in Galilee, Jesus said to them, 'The Son of Man is about to be delivered into the hands of men, and they will kill him, and he will be raised on the third day.' And they were greatly distressed." Jesus repeated this prophecy over and over to his disciples in the same way. The thief was promised that He would be with Jesus again in paradise but not that day. Jesus had a profound work to do before establishing His kingdom.

Another passage sometimes presented during sermons on death revolves around Revelations 6:9-11 which states: "When he opened the fifth seal, I saw under the altar the souls of those who had been slain for the word of God and for the witness they had borne. They cried out with a loud voice, 'O Sovereign Lord, holy and true, how long before you will judge and avenge our blood on those who dwell on the earth?' Then they were each given a white robe and told to rest a little longer, until the number of their fellow servants and their brothers should be complete, who were to be killed as they them-selves had been." The idea here is that there are souls in heaven crying out to God for vengeance on those who took their lives. Are there saints already in heaven who are petitioning God for action? Note that John is seeing a vision, a representation of future events and not reality in any form. The entire chapter is full of symbolism. For example, the second rider is allowed to take peace from the earth, the fourth rider is "death" and "Hades" followed him. Can a horse rider with a great sword end peace on earth? Can death and Hades liter-ally ride a horse? Likewise, the altar with souls under it is a symbol and not the first time this symbol appears in Holy Scripture. Genesis 4:8-11 reads: "Cain spoke to Abel his brother. And when they were in the field, Cain rose up against his brother Abel and killed him. Then the Lord said to Cain, 'Where is Abel your brother?' He said, 'I do not know; am I my brother's keeper?' And the Lord said, "What have you done? The voice of your brother's blood is crying to me from the ground. And now you are cursed from the ground, which has opened its mouth to receive your brother's blood from your hand." In the same way that Abel's blood cried out to God in symbolic form so the blood of His dead saints murdered by those living on the earth are in God's hearing. As the Father brought justice to Cain so He will remember his slain children. In summary, this is not a literal picture of resurrected saints under an altar crying out to God.

Some teachers use Paul's writing in Ephesians 2:5 as a proof of being with Christ upon death. " even when we were dead in our trespasses, made us alive together with Christ—by grace you have been saved— ". Clearly, when taken with the first four verses of this chapter, Paul is not talking about physical death. Instead, he is talking about spiritual death that all people face until Christ makes them alive. Many people are alive physically today but are spiritually dead.

Occasionally I will hear John 11:26 quoted: "and everyone who lives and believes in me shall never die. Do you believe this?" This, according to some, answers the question about immediate after-life. This verse comes from one of the most famous passages in the Bible, specifically when Jesus raised Lazarus from the dead. Here is the full text from John 11:20-27:

"So when Martha heard that Jesus was coming, she went and met him, but Mary remained seated in the house. Martha said to Jesus, 'Lord, if you had been here, my brother would not have died. But even now I know that whatever you ask from God, God will give you.' Jesus said to her, 'Your brother will rise again.' Martha said to him, 'I know that he will rise again in the resurrection on the last day.' Jesus said to her, 'I am the resurrection and the life. Whoever believes in me, though he die, yet shall he live, and everyone who lives and believes in me shall never die. Do you believe this?' She said to him, 'Yes, Lord; I believe that you are the Christ, the Son of God, who is coming into the world.' Notice that Martha says to our Lord "I know that he (Lazarus) will rise again in the resurrection on the last day." Jesus did not refute this comment nor challenge her words in any fashion. Instead he reassures Martha that the words she has spoken are absolutely true. Our Savior says "though he die, yet shall he live" and not just Lazarus but "everyone who lives and believes in [Christ] shall never die". Lazarus was raised from the dead only to die again. Jesus is the true resurrection. All who have believed in Christ "though we die" on this earth will live again at His return never to die.

One of the more interesting and mysterious stories in Scripture occurs in 1st Samuel 28 when King Saul encountered what some call the "Witch of En-dor". Saul was in great distress because Israel's great enemy, the Philistine army, was drawing near for a great battle and Samuel, the judge, prophet and Saul's adviser had died. You can read the entire chapter for the background and results of this encounter between Saul and the necromancer. What is relevant to this discussion is that some say that because Saul's medium was apparently able to bring Samuel back to life is proof that the prophet was alive in heaven or perhaps Sheol, the place of the dead. Here are the key verses in the passage: "11 Then the woman said, 'Whom shall I bring up for you?' He said, 'Bring up Samuel for me.' 12 When the woman saw Samuel, she cried out with a loud voice. And the woman said to Saul, 'Why have you deceived me? You are Saul.' 13 The king said to her, 'Do not be afraid. What do you see?' And the woman said to Saul, 'I see a god coming up out of the earth.' 14 He said to her, 'What is his appearance?' And she said, 'An old man is coming up, and he is wrapped in a robe.' And Saul knew that it was Samuel, and he bowed with his face to the ground and paid homage."

Notice that when the woman saw Samuel, "she cried out with a loud voice." She was frightened because she knew that she had no power to restore life to the dead. This medium was a phony and she knew it. Just like every other person throughout the ages who has claimed to speak to the dead without God's deliberate intervention. Some say this apparition was a demon or Satan himself but I have trouble reconciling that with the truth that Samuel speaks to Saul. Instead, I suggest this Samuel is a vision from God, sent to warn Saul of his impending doom. Notice further that Samuel asks Saul in verse 15: "Why have you disturbed me by bringing me up?" Up from where: the grave, Sheol, hell? Heaven is never described as being down below the earth. The place of God's glory is always pictured as being above this earth. God would never grant authority to Saul or this heathen woman to raise someone from the dead. On the contrary God had ordered Saul to eliminate all witchcraft and medium influence from Israel because He knew they would mislead the people about their ability to speak to those beyond the grave. It is important to note in Scripture that the only people resuscitated (raised from the dead temporarily to die again) came through the power of God. Christ is the only person to have ever been resurrected (raised from the dead to never die again). Again this is only possible through the power of God. Make no mistake about this incident. This woman did not resuscitate the prophet Samuel from the dead. There is no place in the Bible, or in history for that matter, that a human being outside the will and instruction of God, ever heard or saw a formerly dead person alive again. This authority belongs exclusively to God.

But what about when Jesus says in Matthew 22:31-32: "And as for the resurrection of the dead, have you not read what was said to you by God: 'I am the God of Abraham, and the God of Isaac, and the God of Jacob?' He is not God of the dead, but of the living?'" Is Jesus saying that the dead are now living? Look carefully at the exact phrasing as for the resurrection of the dead to understand the Lord's position. Jesus was speaking to Sadducees the largest sect of Jewish believers of His era. These men did not believe in the resurrection of the dead and taught their followers accordingly. Our Savior made it clear to these men and others like them that there will be a resurrection of the dead. All who have ever lived will be resurrected, some to judgment and others to eternal life. The Bible never says that every person that dies will be immediately resurrected; instead Scripture is consistent throughout in saying that the dead will be raised on The Day of the Lord when Christ returns.

A few authors have tried to use the enigmatic verses in Hebrews 12:18-24 to say that believers are living in heaven now. This chapter is one of the most debated and discussed in all of Scripture and I am skeptical about building a theology from these words. Instead, what is clear is that the author is drawing a contrast between the Old Covenant between God and Moses at Mt Sinai to the New Covenant of grace derived from the shed blood of Jesus Christ. These verses do not even loosely imply that believers are immediately carried away into heaven.

Lastly, some will say "what about the transfiguration?" Weren't there two resurrected souls with Jesus on a high mountain? The last verse of Matthew chapter 16 Jesus says: "Truly, I say to you, there are some standing here who will not taste death until they see the Son of Man coming in his kingdom." And true to His word, just six days later, Jesus invited Peter, James, and John to see a preview of the kingdom of heaven. Matthew 17:1-3 and following describe one of the most remarkable events in Scripture. "Jesus took with him Peter and James, and John his brother, and led them up a high mountain by themselves. And he was transfigured before them, and his face shone like the sun, and his clothes became white as light. And behold, there appeared to them Moses and Elijah, talking with him."

There are two mainstream theories about this event. The first is stated in verse 9 when Jesus says to his disciples: "And as they were coming down the mountain, Jesus commanded them, 'Tell no one the vision, until the Son of Man is raised from the dead.' Much like John's vision in Revelations and Daniel's vision in the Old Testament, some say that God showed the disciples a vision of the second coming where Christ would be joined in the sky with the dead saints (represented by Moses) and those living (represented by Elijah). You may recall that Elijah never died but was translated via a whirlwind into heaven. The other theory is that Christ was indeed joined by two men, Moses and Elijah. Two men not disembodied souls, spirits or ghosts. As mentioned before, Elijah never died. Moses, "died and was buried" but "no one knows the place of his burial to this day" so says Deuteronomy 34:5-6. There is also an interesting verse in Jude, the one chapter book in the New Testament that says in verse 9: "But when the archangel Michael, contending with the devil, was disputing about the body of Moses, he did not presume to pronounce a blasphemous judgment, but said, 'The Lord rebuke you.'" Some believe Moses was raised, the devil objected, and Michael rebuked Satan. In either case, whether simply a vision or two men appeared with Christ, the illustration is the same. Jesus gave his disciples a glimpse of His future coming kingdom. The Bible does not say two resurrected souls joined Jesus from heaven.

So far we have evaluated what the Bible does not say about death. What does it say? Here are some examples:

Ecclesiastes 9:5 – "For the living know that they will die, but the dead know nothing, and they have no more reward, for the memory of them is forgotten".

Ecclesiastes 9:10 – "Whatever your hand finds to do, do it with your might, for there is no work or thought or knowledge or wisdom in Sheol, to which you are going."

Job 14:12 – "so a man lies down and rises not again; till the heavens are no more he will not awake or be roused out of his sleep."

Psalm 115:17 – "The dead do not praise the Lord, nor do any who go down into silence."

Psalm 146:4 – "When his breath departs, he returns to the earth; on that very day his plans perish."

Acts 2:29 – "Brothers, I may say to you with confidence about the patriarch David that he both died and was buried, and his tomb is with us to this day." Followed closely by

Acts 2:34 – "For David did not ascend into the heavens..."

Simply put, the dead are dead. There is no "soul sleep". When someone dies, the body, soul, and spirit are dead. But there is glorious news—there will be a resurrection of the dead when Christ returns.

Here's what the Bible says:

John 5:28-29 – "Do not marvel at this, for an hour is coming when all who are in the tombs will hear his voice and come out, those who have done good to the resurrection of life, and those who have done evil to the resurrection of judgment."

And when will all come out of the tomb? All will be raised on the last day.

John 6:40 – "For this is the will of my Father, that everyone who looks on the Son and believes in him should have eternal life, and I will raise him up on the last day."

John 6:44 – "No one can come to me unless the Father who sent me draws him. And I will raise him up on the last day."

At His glorious second coming, Jesus will raise all who have died since time began. Yes, that means millions upon millions of human beings will be resurrected. Those who have believed in Christ will receive eternal life. John 6:40 says "everyone who looks on the Son and believes in him should have eternal life". John 3:16 says "For God so loved the world, that he gave his only begotten son that whosoever believeth in him should not perish but have everlasting life (KJV)." In 1 John 2:25 the apostle writes: "And this is the promise that he made to us — eternal life." And 1 Thessalonians 4:17 as Paul describes the second coming: "Then we who are alive, who are left, will be caught up together with them in the clouds to meet the Lord in the air, and so we will always be with the Lord."

The Bible is clear on this topic. Despite the rhetoric and flowery words spoken at funerals, memorial services and during many sermons on the subject of death, those who have died remain dead until Christ returns. At that point, Jesus made clear that every human being will be made alive again. Those who have believed will be granted eternal life by our gracious Savior. We need not fear death because our "breath of life" is held safely and securely by our heavenly father until the last day.

CHAPTER 5

HELL IS A PLACE OF ETERNAL TORMENT FOR UNBELIEVERS

As a youngster I was a latch-key kid. You know the type. My dad died when I was a toddler and my mother worked full-time at a retail store downtown and didn't get home until well after dark. So, every day when I got home from school I would drop off my books and head out into the neighborhood for an adventure. I had no adult supervision and as long as I didn't get in trouble with the law or the neighbors my mom didn't object to whatever I did. Sometimes I would walk a few miles to wander through some retail establishments (those were days before the mall), ride my bike, explore vacant houses, run down the railroad tracks behind our house, hang out at the drugstore, or just visit a friend. It was on one of those typical afternoons that I had my introduction to one worldview of hell.

One of my buddies, Russell by name, was a strange chap who lived in a giant pre-civil war house down the street. On this particular day, I decided to knock on his door and see what mischief the two of us could find. It so happened on this day that Russell was looking through a large print book that had some fascinating pictures. The book's title escapes me but the subject matter was all about Greek mythology's view of the subterranean realm called hades or hell.

Some photos were so graphic in nature I still remember them to this day. One photo showed a man in a flaming lake of fire trying to reach a tree limb to pull himself out of the torment. The tree, unfortunately for him, was just out of his reach. Another picture showed a man being pulled over a rack and stretched beyond the bounds of human endurance. There were various other images of torture in diversified forms. But the one group of photos that are still vivid in my mind was a man in a pool of water with his body below the surface trying to get his head above the water. The next couple of frames showed him gasping for breath and straining to get to the air just inches above his head. Then finally, exhausted and drowning, he fell back deeper into the water but he did not die. The torture all began again. He started straining and gasping for air all over again as he tried to reach the top. This man was in an eternal torture chamber called hell.

While not as explicit as Greek mythology, most modern day teaching views hell as an underground pit of horror where the souls of unbelievers are sent the moment they die. These "souls" are alive, conscious, and are painfully aware of their situation even now. The misery is real and worse, there will never be an end to it. I would estimate that the vast majority of Americans—whether Christian or not—accept as true this premise.

I have heard far too many sermons in my life about an eternal torture chamber called hell. Apparently spurred on by the famous 18th century evangelist Jonathan Edwards and his "Sinners in the Hands of an Angry God" sermon, many modern day preachers and teachers have no compunction about presenting hell as a place of eternal torture and torment for those who have spurned God. Just a few weeks ago at a church where I was visiting, the pastor invited the congregation to come and place names of lost loved ones and friends on a makeshift cross. He gave a lengthy dissertation on the suffering and torment that these people would endure forever if they were sent to hell. His words were intended to stir the listeners to action, to witness to these people before God punished them in unspeakable pain for eternity. The risk of an eternity in the dark abyss has been the tool of "hell fire and damnation" evangelism for centuries.

Virtually all mainstream theologians and churches teach eternal suffering for the unbeliever. There are hundreds of examples. Go to almost any church website to confirm this truth. Look under the tab that says "Statement of Faith" or "What We Believe" and you will read something like this:

"The real you will never die. One day your body will be cremated or buried but your soul, the real you, will live somewhere forever. Either you will exist in heaven with God or separated from God in hell."

Here is another with slight variations:

Heaven and hell are actual places. Those who have accepted Christ as Savior in this life will have eternal life with God in heaven forever. All others will stand in judgment for their sin and will be condemned to everlasting torment and separation from God in hell.

These are not copied from any actual church but are a paraphrase of what I have read at websites published by dozens of churches from many denominations.

The teaching that non-believers at the moment of death will suffer in torment and pain for eternity is so pervasive that one must assume there are dozens of verses in Scripture that support this teaching. Let's investigate what the Bible says about hell.

Let's begin with the thesis that an unbeliever goes immediately to hell at death. What are the Bible verses that support this thinking? Simply put, there are none. Not one place in the Bible does Scripture even hint that when a person dies his soul, or his being, or his consciousness, or his person, or his spirit, or his body, or anything else representing the person immediately descends into hell. You may recall from earlier chapters in this book what the Bible does say about a person's destination at death. In the Old Testament the Hebrew word was Sheol, the place of the dead. The New Testament counterpart in the Greek is Hades, the place of the dead. These words essentially mean the same thing. When a person dies they go to the place of the dead, back to the dust from which the body was formed. Genesis 3:19: "By the sweat of your face you shall eat bread, till you return to the ground, for out of it you were taken; for you are dust, and to dust you shall return." There are many verses in Scripture that emphasize this same truth. (c.f. Job 10:9; Isaiah 29:16; Isaiah 45:9; 2 Corinthians 15:47) The most common usage of these terms is represented by our English word, grave. When someone dies, they go to the grave; that is back to dust. Knowing this, it is difficult to imagine that many people believe that Cain, Achan, Nebuchadnezzar, all those who drowned in the worldwide flood and millions of others that lived in Old Testament times have been suffering in hell since they died thousands of years ago.

There are three words that are translated as hell in the English Bible, all of them in the New Testament. Three Greek words: tartaroo, Hades, and Gehenna. Let's begin with the first one, tartaroo, that appears only once in Scripture in 2 Peter 2:4: "For if God did not spare angels when they sinned, but cast them into hell (tartaroo) and committed them to chains of gloomy darkness to be kept until the judgment;" According to The Expository Dictionary of Bible Words tartaroo means "to confine in Tartaros". This verse states that God has cast down wicked angels into an ominous place called Tartaros until He brings about some future judgment. The Book of Jude substantiates Peter's remarks in verse 6: "And the angels who did not stay within their own position of authority, but left their proper dwelling, he has kept in eternal chains under gloomy darkness until the judgment of the great day—." There are many theories about what these verses actually mean that are beyond the scope of this book. It is enough to say that this definition of hell is about the fate of demons, not about men or their suffering in the afterlife.

The second word, Hades, is the New Testament equivalent of the Old Testament word Sheol, the place of the dead—the grave. Earlier in this book, these words were discussed at length in the chapter about the human soul. Hades is translated hell in some English Bibles like Revelation 6:8 in the KJV which reads: "And I looked, and behold a pale horse: and his name that sat on him was Death, and Hell followed with him." The same is true in the KJV in Revelation 20:14: "And death and hell were cast into the lake of fire." Most other translations use the word Hades instead of hell. The same word, Hades, appears in 1 Corinthians 15:55 in the KJV: "O death, where is thy sting? O grave, where is thy victory?" The word grave is Hades in the original language. Likewise in Acts 2:31 in the KJV: "He seeing this before spake of the resurrection of Christ, that his soul was not left in hell, neither his flesh did see corruption." Again the word for hell is Hades, that is, Christ's soul was not left in the grave and his flesh did not see corruption. All of these passages indicate that Hades is representative of the grave.

The third and final Greek word translated as hell is Gehenna from the Hebrew word Gehinnom. Ancient manuscripts including the Old Testament indicate that Gehenna was a valley just outside the walls of Jerusalem on the southwest side. The place, often called the Valley of the Son of Hinnom in the Old Testament, was known as a garbage dump where fire burned constantly to consume the refuse of the city and surrounding areas. Since the valley was not controlled by Jewish authorities almost anything would be dumped in this place including the bodies of criminals and others who had no suitable burial grounds and dead animals. Fires were built and maintained using sulfur (brimstone) to consume the garbage and carcasses and to hold down the stench that must have permeated the region for miles. This valley is mentioned numerous times in the Old Testament (c.f. Joshua 15:8, 2 Kings 23:10, Jeremiah 7:31) and may have existed for centuries in that same location. Jesus mentioned this place several times including Matthew 5:22: "But I say to you that everyone who is angry with his brother will be liable to judgment; whoever insults his brother will be liable to the council; and whoever says, 'You fool!' will be liable to the hell [Gehenna] of fire." Again in verses 29 and 30 our Lord says: "If your right eye causes you to sin, tear it out and throw it away. For it is better that you lose one of your members than that your whole body be thrown into hell [Gehenna] And if your right hand causes you to sin, cut it off and throw it away. For it is better that you lose one of your members than that your whole body go into hell [Gehenna]".

So in summary, hell is mentioned only in the New Testament and is represented either as Tartaroo, Hades, or Gehenna. Hell is also represented as a fiery place engulfed in real flames. But when do these flames erupt? Let's investigate.

In Matthew 13:40-42 Jesus talks about hell and those destined to go there: "Just as the weeds are gathered and burned with fire, so will it be at the end of the age. The Son of Man will send his angels, and they will gather out of his kingdom all causes of sin and all law-breakers, and throw them into the fiery furnace. In that place there will be weeping and gnashing of teeth. Then the righteous will shine like the sun in the kingdom of their Father. He who has ears, let him hear." The apostle Peter added this comment when discussing scoffers scoffing in the last days: "But by the same word the heavens and earth that now exist are stored up for fire, being kept until the day of judgment and destruction of the ungodly." (2 Peter 3:7) Clearly, those who deny that hell will ever exist as a real place must have a real issue with these verses. When does our Lord (and Peter) say the fire of hell will burn? At the end of the age, that is, at the end of time and our world as we know it. Fire will consume both the heavens and the earth. There are no verses anywhere in Scripture that indicate hell exists today and has for thousands of years.

What will happen on that Day of Judgment when the fire of hell rages? In Revelation 20:15 the apostle John says "And if anyone's name was not found written in the book of life, he was thrown into the lake of fire." The next verse gives us even more insight. Revelation 21:1: "Then I saw a new heaven and a new earth, for the first heaven and the first earth had passed away, and the sea was no more." And then verse 5 of the same chapter is the best news of all: "And he who was seated on the throne said, 'Behold, I am making all things new.' Also he said, 'Write this down, for these words are trustworthy and true.'" And then John writes the conclusion for those without Christ in Revelation 21:8: "But as for the cowardly, the faithless, the detestable, as for murderers, the sexually immoral, sorcerers, idolaters, and all liars, their portion will be in the lake that burns with fire and sulfur, which is the second death (Italics mine)". This time there will be no resurrection of the unsaved. Try to fathom this incredible news, Christ returns for His church and raises both the living and the dead, after which will be the destruction of the wicked, and then our loving Heavenly Father will create a new heaven and a new earth for His beloved children that will last for eternity.

Hymn writers have joined in the chorus of voices about hell (pun intended). Listen carefully for lyrics imploring listeners to beware of hell's power or hell's hosts. Eighteenth century song writers used terms like hell is raging or hell is moving and inscribe Satan as the prince of hell. Hell is often pictured in music as a place where Satan is currently reigning over the dark domain. With an iron fist, the devil rules his mighty empire from some underground base. From there, terrible, dark powers surge across the earth trying to trap believers and encourage the lost to greater heights of sin. Nothing could be further from the truth. Satan is more fearful of hell than most human beings. He knows of the reality and certainty of his destiny there.

The Bible is clear on this matter. Hell will be a real place, a fiery pit created by God for Satan and his followers and for the destruction of the wicked. The lost do not have eternal life; they will die a second death. The Bible does not speak of "eternal dying", or "eternal suffering" or any other such phrase. Listen to these verses beginning in the Old Testament:

- "For behold, the day is coming, burning like an oven, when all the arrogant and all evildoers will be stubble. The day that is coming shall set them ablaze, says the Lord of hosts, so that it will leave them neither root nor branch." (Malachi 4:1) The prophet warns that the wicked will be set ablaze and left as refuse.

- "And you shall tread down the wicked, for they will be ashes under the soles of your feet, on the day when I act, says the Lord of hosts." (Malachi 4:3) The ashes of the wicked will be trodden under foot by the righteous on "the day that is coming".

- "By the multitude of your iniquities,in the unrighteousness of your trade you profaned your sanctuaries; so I brought fire out from your midst; it consumed you, and I turned you to ashes on the earth in the sight of all who saw you. All who know you among the peoples are appalled at you; you have come to a dreadful end and shall be no more forever." (Ezekiel 28:18-19) God promises the unrighteous will be destroyed by fire and shall be no more forever.

- "As smoke is driven away, so you shall drive them away; as wax melts before fire, so the wicked shall perish before God!" (Psalm 68:2)

- "Mark the blameless and behold the upright, for there is a future for the man of peace. But transgressors shall be altogether destroyed; the future of the wicked shall be cut off." (Psalm 37:37-38) There is a bright and wonderful future for people who know the Prince of Peace but the future of the unrighteous is destruction.

- The New Testament and our Savior's own words continue the same theme.

- "For God so loved the world, that he gave his only Son, that whoever believes in him should not perish but have eternal life. (John 3:16). Only those who believe in Christ will be awarded eternal life, all others perish.

- His winnowing fork is in his hand, and he will clear his threshing floor and gather his wheat into the barn, but the chaff he will burn with unquenchable fire." (Matthew 3:12) These are the words of John the Baptist speaking about Jesus.

- "And do not fear those who kill the body but cannot kill the soul. Rather fear him who can destroy both soul and body in hell." (Matthew 10:28) These words were spoken by Christ to His disciples as our Lord sent them out for service. He instructed them to have no fear of any man who can only kill the body but instead fear God who can destroy both soul and body in hell.

- "For the wages of sin is death, but the free gift of God is eternal life in Christ Jesus our Lord" (Romans 6:23). Sin has a wage and it is death but the free gift of God is eternal life only for those in Jesus Christ. Paul writes these truths to the burgeoning church in Rome.

- "They will suffer the punishment of eternal destruction, away from the presence of the Lord and from the glory of his might" (2 Thessalonians 1:9). Paul tells the church at Thessalonica that "when the Lord Jesus is revealed from heaven with his mighty angels in flaming fire" those who do not know God will face eternal destruction.

- "But the day of the Lord will come like a thief, and then the heavens will pass away with a roar, and the heavenly bodies will be burned up and dissolved, and the earth and the works that are done on it will be exposed [burned up according to the oldest manuscripts]" (2 Peter 3:10)

Scripture is consistent about this subject. Malachi, Ezekiel, the Psalmist, Jesus, Paul, Matthew, Peter and John all say the same thing. Those who do not know God will be utterly destroyed forever. There are no verses that indicate "eternal souls" will reside in a place called hell in terrible pain and suffering forever. There are no references to "eternal dying" or of decades, centuries, and eons of torture at the hands of a righteous God. Perish means perish not perishing. If people were going to suffer endlessly in a torture chamber called hell, I'm convinced God would have told us so plainly and in so many verses they would fill a library.

So besides poets, artists and scholars of the Middle Ages who taught a theory of everlasting torment for unbelievers, what Bible verses do some theologians and teachers use today to support this position?

- "And another angel, a third, followed them, saying with a loud voice, 'If anyone worships the beast and its image and receives a mark on his forehead or on his hand, he also will drink the wine of God's wrath, poured full strength into the cup of his anger, and he will be tormented with fire and sulfur in the presence of the holy angels and in the presence of the Lamb. And the smoke of their torment goes up forever and ever, and they have no rest, day or night, these worshipers of the beast and its image, and whoever receives the mark of its name.'" (Revelation 14:9-11). These verses full of symbolism of a third angel, the beast, and the cup of God's anger say that worshipers of the beast will be tormented with fire and sulfur and the "smoke of their torment goes up forever and ever". Whether or not worshipers of the beast represents the lost since the beginning of time is subject to debate especially when John tells us later in the book the unrighteous are cast into the lake of fire and experience the second death. Even in the unlikely event this represents the unsaved masses of mankind, the image is of separation from God forever. That is, their destruction will separate them from God, loved ones, and friends for eternity. There is no rest, no reconciliation, no resurrection—their existence is extinguished.

- "And these will go away into eternal punishment, but the righteous into eternal life" (Matthew 25:46). Christ uses the picture of those who gave him no food, no drink, did not welcome him, clothe him or visit him in prison, a picture of those who reject our Lord in this life. What will be their reward? Eternal punishment. That is everlasting separation from God, loved ones, and friends with no appeal, hope of acquittal, or second chance. The Lord did not use terms such as eternal punishing, eternal suffering, eternal torment, eternal torture or any other such expressions.

- "And if your eye causes you to sin, tear it out. It is better for you to enter the kingdom of God with one eye than with two eyes to be thrown into hell, 'where their worm does not die and the fire is not quenched'" (Mark 9:47-48). The imagery of the worm and fire is clearly taken from Isaiah 66:24 where the prophet is describing the events as the Messiah establishes his kingdom. God has triumphed and the Messiah's enemies have been overcome. These enemies of God are slain in such great numbers that the worm (i.e. the worm eating the dead flesh) would be able to live a very long time because of the quantity of defeated foes. Likewise, Isaiah said the fire that was used to consume the bodies would be enormous in size. Jesus builds upon Isaiah's word picture. The Lord's image is of great misery as well as certain and terrible destruction. There obviously would not be worms in hell that could survive in fervent heat. The Lord is using "their worm does not die" and "fire is not quenched" to represent the massive number of God's enemies who will be brought to justice on The Day of Judgment.

• "Then he will say to those on his left, 'Depart from me, you cursed, into the eternal fire prepared for the devil and his angels'" (Matthew 25:41). The fire doesn't burn eternally; the destruction the fire causes lasts forever. How do I know this? Read the one chapter Book of Jude, Verse 7: "just as Sodom and Gomorrah and the surrounding cities, which likewise indulged in sexual immorality and pursued unnatural desire, serve as an example by undergoing a punishment of eternal fire." Sodom and Gomorrah were wicked cities destroyed by God with fire from heaven. The cities and every living thing inside them were obliterated by God's wrath. The author used the term "eternal fire" and yet we know that the fire of those cities is not ablaze today. But, the utter destruction is eternal. The punishment lasts forever but not the flame. Peter's second epistle says the same thing. In 2 Peter 2:6, the apostle says "if by turning the cities of Sodom and Gomorrah to ashes he condemned them to extinction, making them an example of what is going to happen to the ungodly". Peter told his readers that God condemned the residents of Sodom and Gomorrah to ashes, to complete and utter ruin as "an example of what is going to happen to the ungodly". All of these verses remind us that God's judgment fire is forever. The destruction is forevermore.

Some teachers use the parable of Lazarus and the rich man to be an example of an eternal hell. Since I have dedicated an entire chapter of this book on that subject, I would encourage the reader to refer to those comments. Suffice to say that this parable, when taken in context with the others around it, was a clear condemnation of the Scribes and Pharisees and their hypocritical view of God. It has nothing to do with heaven or hell.

Hell is going to be a real place. Hell will be a lake of fire created by God to destroy His enemies. Theologians who choose not to believe in hell choose not to believe Scripture. It is an awful and fearful place that must be avoided at all costs. The punishment those going there will receive is forever without any second chance. The Bible teaches these truths over and over. But, take heart, those who have put their faith in Jesus Christ will have eternal life. God has promised a new heaven and a new earth made for His people that will continue forever.

CHAPTER 6

THE SIGNS OF THE TIMES INDICATE THE LORD'S RETURN IS IMMINENT

Throughout my adult life I have heard many sermons about prophecy and the end-times. The apocalyptic message usually focuses on the words of Christ in Matthew 24 and the corresponding text in Mark 13 and Luke 21. With some variations, the theme is this: "Expect the return of Christ at any moment because the Bible warns us of certain events that will occur just before His coming that are taking place even as we speak." Books, pamphlets, and tracts are readily available that purportedly make it clear that the signs in these verses are there to alert believers that the Lord's return is imminent. Songs and anthems trumpet what must take place just before the return of Christ.

You may have seen churches present dramas or pageants depicting the return of Christ usually as an alternative to Halloween celebrations. Always in these presentations certain signs occur like weather changes or earthquakes that point to the imminent second coming of our Lord and the destruction of the earth. Those attending the show are challenged to watch for these events in the real world as the true indicators of the immediacy of the Second Advent. The conclusion is always to look at these signs and "know that he is near, at the very gates." (Matthew 24:33)

The events of Matthew 24 take place during "Passion Week", the last week of our Lord's life on this earth. Jesus had already made His triumphal entry into Jerusalem on Sunday and after the temple cleansing on Monday, He spent much of the next two days teaching in the temple. His enemies used the time to debate Christ and to try to trap Him in his words. To fully understand Matthew 24, the reader must take into context the events leading up to this chapter. In Matthew 16:21, Jesus told his disciples: "From that time Jesus began to show his disciples that he must go to Jerusalem and suffer many things from the elders and chief priests and scribes, and be killed, and on the third day be raised." At that point, Jesus' earthly ministry changed to one of conflict with the religious authorities. Prior to this, Christ had instructed those He healed and to whom He ministered to keep quiet about who had blessed them. But as His time of suffering approaches, the Lord warns his disciples over and over about the confrontation to take place in Jerusalem. He became bold in his attacks on the religious leaders and sharply criticized their hypocrisy in very public places. Here are a few of these clashes:

a) At the Feast of Dedication (aka Hanukkah) just a few weeks before Passion Week, Jesus told the religious leaders in John 10:30: "I and the Father are one." His Jewish opponents picked up stones to kill him. Christ's claim that He and God are the same enraged his enemies.

b) Two months before Palm Sunday, Jesus returned to Bethany (a village 2 miles from Jerusalem) and raised Lazarus from the dead. You know the story. Jesus was already at odds with the Pharisees and Sadducees; but from this point, Jesus as well as Lazarus became marked men. The enemies of Christ wanted to kill both of them. It would be dangerous to ever return to Jerusalem. And yet, He returned for the Passover feast.

c) Luke 19:37-40 describes the scene at what many scholars call "The Triumphal Entry": "When he came near the place where the road goes down the Mount of Olives, the whole crowd of disciples began joyfully to praise God in loud voices for all the miracles they had seen: 'Blessed is the king who comes in the name of the Lord!', 'Peace in heaven and glory in the highest!' Some of the Pharisees in the crowd said to Jesus, 'Teacher, rebuke your disciples!' 'I tell you,' he replied, 'if they keep quiet, the stones will cry out.'"

Jesus rode into town on a colt and Jewish pilgrims from all around the world saw and heard His arrival. When the Pharisees tried to silence the crowd, Jesus made it clear that even the stones would shout Hosanna (literally, God save us) if His followers kept quiet. It is clearly evident that Jesus wanted all Jerusalem to know He was there and claiming to be God. So by the time our Lord arrived at Jerusalem for the Passover celebration His enemies were angry and anxious to silence this interloper.

d) Mark 11:15-18 describes the cleansing of the temple on Monday: "And they came to Jerusalem. And he entered the temple and began to drive out those who sold and those who bought in the temple, and he overturned the tables of the money-changers and the seats of those who sold pigeons. And he would not allow anyone to carry anything through the temple. And he was teaching them and saying to them, 'Is it not written, My house shall be called a house of prayer for all the nations'? But you have made it a den of robbers.' And the chief priests and the scribes heard it and were seeking a way to destroy him, for they feared him, because all the crowd was astonished at his teaching."

This further annoyed and frustrated the religious leaders because Christ had driven their profit making from the temple and then returned and began teaching in that very place. The setting is complete. The Jewish people are thrilled and eager for a word from God while their leaders, the scribes and Pharisees, are furious and seeking Jesus' death.

It is with that backdrop that Chapter 23 begins. Jesus is preaching, teaching, and healing in the temple while debating with His enemies. In this chapter, Jesus sharply criticizes the teachers of the law and the Pharisees. Jesus talked about God sending them prophets, wise men and teachers some of whom they would kill and crucify. Others they would flog, persecute, and pursue from town to town. He called them harsh names: hypocrites, brood of vipers, blind guides, fools, white-washed tombs and serpents. He asked them "how are you to escape being sentenced to hell (Gehenna)?" The tension between our Lord and these men was enormous and the disciples must have been wondering about all of this. Was Jesus about to take control as Messiah? Use your mind's eye to put yourself in the place of Christ's disciples. They are stunned and perhaps even traumatized by the vitriol with which the Lord addresses the religious leaders. In today's world it would be like Christ chastising the Pope or Billy Graham, men we have been taught to respect since childhood.

Then as Jesus prepares to leave the temple He comments about Jerusalem in Matthew 23:37-39: "O Jerusalem, Jerusalem, the city that kills the prophets and stones those who are sent to it! How often would I have gathered your children together as a hen gathers her brood under her wings, and you would not! See, your house is left to you desolate. For I tell you, you will not see me again, until you say, 'Blessed is he who comes in the name of the Lord.'" The Jews religious house was utterly worthless and after this point Jesus did not enter the temple again.

Chapter 24 then begins with verses 1 and 2: "Jesus left the temple and was going away, when his disciples came to point out to him the buildings of the temple. But he answered them, 'You see all these, do you not? Truly, I say to you, there will not be left here one stone upon another that will not be thrown down.'"

Luke's parallel account continues this discussion in Chapter 21, verse 7: "And they asked him, "Teacher, when will these things be, and what will be the sign when these things are about to take place?" Matthew's account differs slightly with the question in 24:3 being: "Tell us, when will these things be, and what will be the sign of your coming and of the close of the age?" It is important to remember that Matthew was writing to Jews to convince the Jewish people that their long awaited Messiah had come. Matthew's account is written carefully and with great detail from a Jewish perspective. It would be natural for the disciples when asking this question to assume that Jesus was about to establish His kingdom on this earth. Their question regarding "the sign of your coming and of the close of the age" does not refer to Christ's second coming as we understand it today. They know nothing, at this point, of a second advent of Christ. Instead, they believe Christ is about to begin His rule as Messiah, to overthrow Roman rule, and to establish His kingdom in Jerusalem forever. These men believe Christ will save both Israel and the temple, the very dwelling place of God. The Lord's remark that the temple would be destroyed would be very difficult for them to understand. There can be only one of two answers for this conundrum from their understanding of Scripture:

1) That the "time of the end" mentioned in Daniel 8:17; 11:35, 40; and 12:4, 9 was at hand

2) The "abomination of desolation" in Daniel 9:27, 11:31, and 12:11 was going to occur

Jesus clears up the matter later in this chapter.

The disciples are asking three questions in Matthew's account:

a) When will these things be?

b) What will be the sign of your coming?

c) When will the end of the age occur?

It is critical to understand that the Lord answered all three questions individually and very specifically.

First question, when will these things be? The "things" are the events Jesus talked about in verse 2 when He told them the temple would be completely and utterly destroyed. In the verses that follow, the Lord warns them about false prophets and teachers, many of whom will say "I am the Christ" and will lead many astray. He warns of wars and rumors of wars, famines, and earthquakes "but the end is not yet". Jesus tells his disciples that they will be delivered into tribulation and even put to death. What a shocking testimony to men expecting to be immediately elevated to positions of authority in the new kingdom. Many, the Lord says, "will fall away and betray one another and hate one another." He tells them though the love of many will grow cold, "the gospel of the kingdom will be proclaimed throughout the whole world." Jesus then specifically tells His disciples that He is referring to Daniel's "abomination of desolation" when he says in verses 15 and 16: "So when you see the abomination of desolation spoken of by the prophet Daniel, standing in the holy place (let the reader understand), then let those who are in Judea flee to the mountains." Our Lord said "so when you see" the "you" can only be his disciples, his listeners, those men standing with Him at that moment. He is warning them that they will see the abomination of desolation in their lifetimes. He goes on to say in verse 20 when the desolation arrives: "Pray that your flight may not be in winter or on a Sabbath." Most Christians don't worship on the Sabbath; they worship on the first day of the week, the Lord's Day as a weekly celebration of the resurrection. Then why would the Lord make this statement if he is addressing Christians who will live far in the future? Clearly He is saying to those with Jewish backgrounds, "I know you can't travel far on the Sabbath because of what you think the law demands, so you had better hope this desolation isn't on a Sabbath day so you can flee far and fast." Jesus continues by saying that the tribulation is so great that: "if those days had not been cut short, no human being would be saved. But for the sake of the elect those days will be cut short." Our Savior then makes His most critical statement about these "things" in verse 34: "Truly, I say to you, <u>this generation will not pass away until all these things take place</u>." (Emphasis mine). Every bit of evidence in this discussion indicates that Jesus is talking about the temple's destruction in A.D. 70 by Rome. History tells us that Jews and Christians alike suffered immeasurably under the iron fist of Rome and specifically the armies of Titus during this time of persecution. This is validated by the context of the entire chapter, the disciples' specific question about the temple's destruction, the fact that "this generation will not pass away until all these things take place", and Luke's parallel account, "when you see Jerusalem sur-rounded by armies, then know that its desolation has come near." All of these events are signs of Jerusalem's imminent destruction at the hand of Rome in AD 70, not the second coming of Christ. Jesus has clearly answered question 1, "when will these things be"?

Second question, what will be the sign of your coming? Again, His disciples would not have known anything about a second com-ing. Their expectations probably included the end of gentile rule and the glory of Israel being established as so many Old Testament verses predicted (c.f. 1 Samuel 15:29; Ezekiel 8:4; Isaiah 60:1). However, with the destruction of Jerusalem and the temple in A.D. 70 many in the early Christian church must have thought that the return of Christ was imminent. Jesus said there will be a sign of his coming.

Beginning in verse 29 Jesus speaks: "Immediately after the tribulation of those days the sun will be darkened, and the moon will not give its light, and the stars will fall from heaven, and the powers of the heavens will be shaken. Then will appear in heaven the <u>sign</u> of the Son of Man, and then all the tribes of the earth will mourn, <u>and they will see the Son of Man coming on the clouds of heaven with power and great glory.</u> And he will send out his angels with a loud trumpet call, and they will gather his elect from the four winds, from one end of heaven to the other." (Emphasis mine). The sign is His second coming and nothing else. In other words, there are no advance signs Christians should be watching that predict the coming of our Lord.

The third question, when will the end of the age occur? Verse 36 answers this question directly,

"But concerning that day and hour no one knows, not even the angels of heaven, nor the Son, but the Father only." Acknowledge this as the truth and everything else falls into place. Jesus is not prophesying about the time of his second coming because He made it clear that even He did not know the day or the hour. Instead, the Lord says in verse 42: "Therefore, stay awake, for you do not know on what day your Lord is coming. But know this, that if the master of the house had known in what part of the night the thief was coming, he would have stayed awake and would not have let his house be broken into. Therefore you also must be ready, for the Son of Man is coming at an hour you do not expect." Put succinctly, Jesus said don't watch for signs or worldly events that predict His coming. Instead, live as if His return will be today. Be ready because Christ will return when you do not expect Him.

What can we know for sure? The words of Jesus were clear and to the point. Nobody knows when Christ is coming again and, for that reason, we should be living each day as if it were today. Don't be watching for worldly events or signs because there are no clues to be had there. Read the Bible for what it says and don't try to piece together random verses with random theories to build a theology that is not Biblical. In Matthew 24:29 Jesus used the term "immediately" to reflect when the Sign of His return would occur though He Himself did not know the exact date and time. I take the meaning of immediately as it could happen at any moment. Believe that God has the perfect timing in mind for our Savior's return and do your best to be prepared. Even so, come quickly Lord Jesus.

CHAPTER **7**

IN CASE OF RAPTURE, THIS VEHICLE WILL BE UNMANNED

One of the most prevalent teachings in today's evangelical church-es is the doctrine of a pre-tribulation rapture of the church of Jesus Christ. The rapture principle says that Jesus will someday return to earth in the sky and call all of His followers, both living and dead, to join Him in heaven. The result is that only non-Christians will remain on the earth to face seven (or perhaps three and one-half) years of tribulation and peril. After the terrible great tribulation, Christ returns again with His saints to destroy his enemies, judge mankind, and set up His 1000 year reign.

This theology is so important in most mainstream churches today that books, pamphlets, tracts, Sunday school lessons, and sermons are routinely offered on this subject as Biblical truth. Several weeks ago I was visiting a church where the pastor's message was entitled "Seven Things You Should Know". The fifth of the seven "things" he said "the Bible says that Jesus will come and rapture His church away and then gloriously return seven years later with His people to estab-lish His kingdom". There was no language like "I believe that…." or "Some Bible scholars believe that…" there is a rapture. It was "THE BIBLE SAYS"! Well, um, no it doesn't. I've read the Bible cover to cover and there are no verses that state those facts. If someone tells me "the Bible says" I want them to have chapter and verse ready.

Fictional novels describing the lives and events of those still living on the earth after the rapture became best sellers. One church in my neighborhood once posted the following sign over the building's entrance: "We are a fundamental, Bible believing, pre-tribulation, premillennial fellowship." This partial statement of faith would certainly discourage someone from attending who may hold a different viewpoint. Many authors and preachers in the media trumpet their studies of prophecy with the rapture as the centerpiece. At most churches the study of eschatology (end times) begins with what is believed to be the next significant act of God: the rapture of the Christian church.

If so many fundamental, charismatic, and evangelical churches believe and actively teach about the rapture, what Bible passages give credence to such a claim? Most start with Paul's writing to the church at Thessalonica when he says in 1 Thessalonians 4:13-18:

The Coming of the Lord

13 But we do not want you to be uninformed, brothers, about those who are asleep, that you may not grieve as others do who have no hope. 14 For since we believe that Jesus died and rose again, even so, through Jesus, God will bring with him those who have fallen asleep. 15 For this we declare to you by a word from the Lord, that we who are alive, who are left until the coming of the Lord, will not precede those who have fallen asleep. 16 For the Lord himself will descend from heaven with a cry of command, with the voice of an archangel, and with the sound of the trumpet of God. And the dead in Christ will rise first. 17 Then we who are alive, who are left, will be caught up together with them in the clouds to meet the Lord in the air, and so we will always be with the Lord. 18 Therefore encourage one another with these words.

The key phrase to those who believe this passage describes the rapture is "caught up together with them in the clouds to meet the

Lord in the air". According to many theologians (and some of my family members), the rapture will take place in the air while the second coming of Christ will be to the earth to judge the nations. To them, this means there are two separate, distinct returns. One is the rapture when Christ calls His church home and the other, presumably seven years later, His glorious second coming. Unfortunately for those who espouse this argument there is no Biblical evidence that any particular time lapses between the time Christ meets his saints in the sky and He returns to earth. Let me repeat myself for emphasis. Nowhere in Scripture is it indicated that there is a seven year gap—or any period of time—between the "catching away of believers" and then a second coming that begins a general judgment. The fact is that Peter, Paul, and John never mention what would clearly be one of the most dramatic and influential doctrines in the Bible—that Christ is actually returning twice at two separate times.

Instead, some theologians and teachers have chosen to ascribe to the notion that the rapture is a "secret" return before the actual second coming of Christ. And yet, Paul clearly states in Chapter 4 that the Lord Himself will descend from heaven with a CRY OF COMMAND, with the VOICE OF AN ARCHANGEL, and with the SOUND OF THE TRUMPET OF GOD. (Emphasis mine). Paul is explicit in explaining that this event is anything but secret. A shout, a loud voice, and a trumpet announce the Lord's return. The world is loudly and publicly informed of our great God's intervention.

Some who believe in the rapture go further by continuing in 1 Thessalonians to Chapter 5, verse 2 which says "For you yourselves are fully aware that the day of the Lord will come like a thief in the night." The comment about "thief in the night" indicates to them that the rapture is a surprise to the world, not foretold in the Bible by any prophets or signs. However, continue the thought in the very next verse of the same chapter: "While people are saying, 'There is peace and security,' then sudden destruction will come upon them as

labor pains come upon a pregnant woman, and they will not escape."
Here, Paul is clearly talking about the judgment of mankind that is
always mirrored in the second coming of Christ. It is without question
that at this point the enemies of God are destroyed, not seven years
in the future. Furthermore, "the day of the Lord" appearing in verse 2
is consistently applied throughout the New Testament as the Day of
Judgment simultaneous with the Lord's return.

Here are a few examples of the day of the Lord always appearing
as the Day of Judgment.

- Acts 2:17-21 quotes the Old Testament Book of Joel Chapter
  2:28-32 in describing the day of the Lord as: "the sun shall
  be turned to darkness and the moon to blood, before the day
  of the Lord comes, the great and magnificent day." It is unlikely the earth would continue 7 more years under those
  circumstances.

- In Revelation 6:12-17 John describes that day: "there was a
  great earthquake, and the sun became black as sackcloth, the
  full moon became like blood, and the stars of the sky fell to
  the earth as the fig tree sheds its winter fruit when shaken by
  a gale". He goes on to say the wicked call "to the mountains
  and rocks, 'Fall on us and hide us from the face of him who
  is seated on the throne, and from the wrath of the Lamb, for
  the great day of their wrath has come, and who can stand?'"

- The Gospel of Matthew in Chapter 29:30-31 says "Then will
  appear in heaven the sign of the Son of Man, and then all the
  tribes of the earth will mourn, and they will see the Son of
  Man coming on the clouds of heaven with power and great
  glory. And he will send out his angels with a loud trumpet
  call, and they will gather his elect from the four winds, from
  one end of heaven to the other."

In every case the day of the Lord is described as a Day of Judgment or Day of Wrath. Sounds exactly like the event described in 1 Thessalonians Chapters 4 and 5.

The argument is also put forth by those who teach a rapture to use 1 Thessalonians 5:9 to support their position: "For God has not destined us for wrath, but to obtain salvation through our Lord Jesus Christ." The belief is that since Christians are not destined for wrath that they must necessarily be removed from this earth before the time of the great tribulation. This great tribulation period is taught as being different from tribulation that results because Christians live in a fallen world. Hardship, persecution, and life's uncertainties are tribulations for people in general and have existed since the beginning of time. However, there is another great tribulation mentioned by Jesus in Matthew 24:21-22: "For then there will be great tribulation, such as has not been from the beginning of the world until now, no, and never will be. And if those days had not been cut short, no human being would be saved. But for the sake of the elect those days will be cut short." According to dispensationalists (this term is discussed later in the chapter), believers will be "snatched away" before this time. However, it is clear that Paul is talking about the second coming in 1 Thessalonians 4 and 5. Remember also that chapter and verse designation comes from editors and not from the original manuscript. There is no reason to think Paul changed from the rapture to the second coming (or vice versa) because the chapter changes. Christ returns and calls His church to Himself, judges his enemies, and establishes his reign all in a moment, in the twinkling of an eye. All of these events will occur on "The Day of the Lord". Clearly the great tribulation Jesus discussed has already happened before Christ raises the Church to meet Him in the air and brings judgment on His enemies.

Here then is a practical question. Why would God have to remove His people from the globe to protect them from His wrath? There are numerous places in Scripture where God put a hedge of protection around his people and protected them during devastating events. Here are just a few:

1) When Haman manipulated the King of Persia to issue a decree (a decree that could not be revoked by anyone) that the Jewish nation was to be obliterated on a certain day. God used a woman, Esther, to save his people and avoid the extermination of the Hebrews.

2) When God sent plagues upon Egypt, He protected His people from the horrors that afflicted Pharaoh and his fellow Egyptians.

3) A young shepherd boy stood before a giant almost nine feet in stature to do battle for the nation of Israel. A miracle from God allowed Israel to survive.

4) Shadrach, Meshach, and Abednego faced certain death in a fiery furnace but God decided otherwise. Likewise, Daniel should have died in a lion's den but God intervened on behalf of the one He loved.

My point is that God is an all-powerful being who is not intimidated or flustered by the threats of mankind. He is well able to protect His own during a crisis, even one in which he is sending his wrath against the world. The prophet Isaiah wrote in Chapter 26:20-21: "Come, my people, enter your chambers, and shut your doors behind you; hide yourselves for a little while until the fury has passed by. For behold, the LORD is coming out from his place to punish the inhabitants of the earth for their iniquity, and the earth will disclose the blood shed on it, and will no more cover its slain." To say that God is forced to remove His people from the world to protect them lacks credibility.

Many preachers and teachers cite Revelation 3:10 to support their belief in a pre-tribulation rapture. John writes: "Because you have kept my word about patient endurance, I will keep you from the hour of trial that is coming on the whole world, to try those who dwell on the earth." Once again the premise is that God is promising his saints that He will remove them from this earth during the "hour of trial". Taking one verse and using it as the foundation of such an important doctrine is risky. First, and most obvious, this admonition is addressed to the Church at Philadelphia in the first century. This fellowship is one of seven churches in Asia Minor addressed by John in chapters 2 and 3 of Revelation. Many other statements were made about Philadelphia and six others in those two chapters. Are all of those comments related to an apocalyptic event thousands of years later? For example, the Church at Smyrna is told "Do not fear what you are about to suffer. Behold, the devil is about to throw some of you into prison, that you may be tested, and for ten days you will have tribulation." None of the churches are promised protection from future suffering. Are we to choose one verse addressed to one church as "proof" of this doctrine but assume all of the other statements are meant for the first century churches?

Second, the verse is specific "Because you have kept my word....I will keep you...." This is a conditional agreement between the Lord and the Church at Philadelphia specific to those times. Because of your patient endurance, I (God) will act accordingly. God is praising the Philadelphian church for good behavior and rewards them for it. There is no way that this statement can be attributed to worldwide Christian behavior thousands of years later.

Third and finally, the most logical reading of this verse is that God determined to protect His church when the actual persecution and trials of that fellowship occurred soon after receiving this writing. Well documented history shows the early church came under great persecution near the end of the first century that tested the faith of all believers. God promised He would stand with His church and protect them during the ordeal. And He did.

Some scholars claim that each of the five chapters of 1 Thessalonians makes reference to the rapture. In 1 Thessalonians 1:10 the Bible says "and to wait for his Son from heaven, whom he raised from the dead, Jesus who delivers us from the wrath to come." In the second chapter verse 19 Paul writes: "For what is our hope or joy or crown of boasting before our Lord Jesus at his coming? Is it not you?" The next chapter in 3:13 Paul prays: "so that he may establish your hearts blameless in holiness before our God and Father, at the coming of our Lord Jesus with all his saints." Clearly, none of these verses even remotely indicate that a secret rapture will occur before the second coming of Christ. In fact, chapter 4, as we have already seen, promises that believers, both dead and alive at the time of His return, will be caught up to meet Him in the air to return as He establishes His kingdom. "At his coming" and "at the coming of our Lord Jesus" is clear.

The reader by now may be wondering about the 70 weeks of Daniel 9:24. This verse reads: "Seventy weeks are decreed about your people and your holy city, to finish the transgression, to put an end to sin, and to atone for iniquity, to bring in everlasting righteousness, to seal both vision and prophet, and to anoint a most holy place." This verse and several following have been subjects of discussion and debate for years. The dispensational belief is that 69 weeks have been completed and the 70th week is on hold for a great tribulation period between the time of the rapture and Christ's second coming. Other scholars argue that the 70 weeks ended shortly after the time of Paul's conversion. This argument states that the Jews had from AD 30 to AD 70 to accept Christ. When they rejected Jesus, Paul writes in Acts 28:28: "Therefore let it be known to you that this salvation of God has been sent to the Gentiles; they will listen." This was the end of the 70th week. Others say the war on the Jews by Cyrus and Rome beginning in AD 67 and ending in AD 73 is the 70th week. This matches up with the destruction of the temple in AD 70 some 3 ½ years later. Still others say that the Hebrew language is so specific in its unity, in its totality, and in its completeness, that the weeks cannot be split apart to separate a future and final one week. What is the point? I named only a few of dozens of theories about the 70 weeks of Daniel. Nobody should realistically take these verses and build a futuristic theology or otherwise use them as the foundation of their eschatology dogmas.

One other foundation for those who believe in a pre-tribulation rapture is the view that God has two people: 1) Israel and 2) the church of Jesus Christ. The premise is that there are two dispensations. The first is the dispensation of law relating to Israel with animal sacrifices, keeping the commandments, the Jerusalem temple, and all things relating to Judaism. The other dispensation is of grace granted to us by God upon the resurrection of our Lord Jesus. The teaching is that we are living in the dispensation of grace and that the two dispensations cannot coexist. So, the church of Jesus Christ must be raptured so that God can save His people Israel. This thinking makes dispensation theology greater than God's ability to save His own. Every person who has or ever will know God does so by His grace through faith. Romans 4:1-3 says this of Abraham: "What then shall we say was gained by Abraham, our forefather according to the flesh? For if Abraham was justified by works, he has something to boast about, but not before God. For what does the Scripture say? 'Abraham believed God, and it was counted to him as righteousness.'" Hebrews chapter 11 talks about the faith of Abel, Enoch, Noah, Abraham, and others who knew God. Here's the bottom line: Abraham believed God and God declared him righteous. Abraham and all others that God has declared righteous came to God the same way you and I do. Not by works of righteousness or keeping the law or in anything other than God's grace through faith. God doesn't need to rapture His church so that He can begin a new work with Israel. He is not bound by man's dogma about dispensations. God saves Jews and Gentiles alike and He does it everyday.

For one final moment, let's look at the matter logically. What would be the purpose of a rapture? We've already seen that God is able to protect His people during a worldwide tribulation. Jesus doesn't need His followers to return seven years later to establish His kingdom and execute his judgments. Our loving Father is not bound by mankind's doctrines about dispensations. By His grace, He saves all who have faith. Furthermore, many people believe that when a saved person dies they go immediately to heaven to be with Christ and loved ones who have passed before. If this were true, why does the rapture need to occur at all since presumably all deceased believers are already with Christ? Why would the "dead in Christ rise first?" Simply put, there are no verses in Scripture that provide reasons or explanations for Jesus to return more than once. Did God put this "revelation of the rapture" in His word so that only a few who have special discernment can see it and teach it? The answer is unequivocally no.

None of the authors in the New Testament talked about "rapture" or multiple appearances by Christ. Not Paul, Peter, James, John, and not Jesus Himself. And yet, to believe in the rapture has become a test of orthodoxy in many of the churches I have attended in recent years. It is not taught in the Bible and shouldn't be taught or believed by Christians today and certainly never presented as "the Bible says the church will be raptured ….."

This should not sadden or distress us. Instead, rejoice that Christ is coming for His own. Take heart that He will appear in the sky with the voice of the archangel and the trumpet of God and call His church, the living and the dead, to be with Him forever. Know that at His glorious return, we will be changed in a moment, in the twinkling of an eye, from corruptible to incorruptible. "And so shall we ever be with the Lord" is more than just a phrase—it is our hope now and forever. Even so, Lord Jesus, come quickly.

CHAPTER **8**

THE CHURCH IS A POWERFUL INFLUENCE ON THE MODERN WORLD

I'm in a very dark room with people all around me. The noise is deafening. Smoke billows up toward the ceiling from an unknown source. There are multi-colored lights piercing the darkness up ahead. There seems to be a stage up front with a group of folks milling around and a few are holding musical instruments. The sign outside says: "Rock music – Just for You". Someone is playing the bass so loud that my heart is threatening to jump out of rhythm. A guy begins to chant or sing an unfamiliar tune. Most of the people around me are staring at the ceiling or at the floor and a few are lighting up the area by sending messages with their smart phone. Despite the exhortations of the guy singing for the audience to join in, only a handful of people are trying to mouth the words. Even after 15 times the words and melody of the song remains unfamiliar to the listeners. A few folks are talking to their neighbors in shrill voices over the din of noise. The racket is unbearable. Where am I?

No, I'm not at the newest hip club that just opened downtown. And no, it's not the local pub where I've gathered with a group of friends. You may have already guessed that this is one of a multitude of churches across America that seems to exist for trendy young people. This church has no steeple, there is no cross in sight any-where, and if there is a baptistery it is hidden very well. Instead, the building is filled with abstract art, giant posters with the fellowship's brand new stylish logo, and flat-screen televisions blast the latest news of upcoming events. After the music time, the pastor stands before the congregation in jeans and a modish shirt sometimes with beads around his neck. His conversation is folksy, friendly, and mod-ern enough to let everyone listening know that he is familiar with and living today's pop culture.

Down the street another church has been built with a more tra-ditional look. A large steeple sits atop the sanctuary and inside there is a cross in the baptistery behind the pulpit and above the choir loft. Traditional hymns are sung with the occasional chorus and the preacher is dressed in his Sunday-best suit as is most of the congre-gation. The church is half-full and the pastor's message dry as dust. Several of the choir members look like they're asleep and the listeners barely stir until the call for the invitation.

Across town at another church a young minister is stirring up the crowd with a message titled "Things You Should Know". Unfortunately most of the "things", while worthwhile, don't have anything to do with Scripture. Jesus hasn't been mentioned in six weeks.

Further down, at another building, a speaker is working up a sweat preaching the "name it – claim it" doctrine that the Bible purportedly teaches. The belief is that all Christians will be healthy, wealthy, and wise if they are in the will of God. God apparently wants all of His followers to be rich.

At the next stop the church is full as the leader teaches an encour-aging message that people can overcome any problem in life with a positive spirit and willing attitude. Everything said is optimistic and uplifting week after week and nary will a negative comment ever be made here.

The leader at the next fellowship is a great story teller and shares many heartwarming anecdotes about people he has met during his life. No need to ever bring the Bible here.

At the next stop, the speaker says "I", "me", "mine", and "my" dozens of times during the message as she relates her life experiences and how they should be used as a pattern of living for all the attendees. God may be mentioned in passing or as an after-thought.

Politics is the topic at the next gathering. Each Sunday the discussion is about civil rights or political decisions happening in Washington, D.C. or at the state house. What the government needs to do next is almost always the main theme.

One other is the "emerging church", the postmodern phenomenon created almost exclusively for young people and more accurately those of Generation X. Churches describing themselves as the emerging church have sprung up around the USA. In this church, no theology or doctrine is final and accepted as truth. The general philosophy seems to be "Here's what I believe but I could be wrong. What's your idea?" There are no absolutes in these fellowships. The group tends to embrace youth culture and strives to be creative in its worship services. For example, many emerging church meetings forego preaching a Bible message to more inventive approaches such as watching movies, listening to soft music, doing creative art or poetry, or journaling.

If you have attended more than one church in your life, you probably have been to some of these churches. You may even attend one right now. In recent years I have visited a large number of churches to the point that I tease my wife by saying we're going to 52 different churches the next 52 weeks. I am greatly distressed with the Christian church's impact in this world. And I am certainly not alone. People are leaving organized worship in droves. Look at the results of this recent survey from Sermancentral.com:

- Only 17.5% of the population of the US attends church on a regular Sunday.

- During the 1990's there was a 19.4% decline in church attendance.

- 85% of churches in America are plateaued or declining.

- Only 12% of children raised in Bible Believing churches stay in the church after age 18.

Worldwide the results are even worse. Check any credible survey on the Internet on church attendance and you'll find that fewer than 1 in 5 people attend weekly worship in Europe. Less than 10% of the population attends any church in Belgium, Norway, Denmark, Sweden, and Finland. This decline has been both gradual and consistent for years. The surveys indicate that boredom and lack of motivation are the leading reasons stated for the decline in the Protestant church. Catholics have the same reasons and add a third: negative media coverage of scandals within the church.

The decline in church attendance not only represents fewer people in the pews but also means the Christian church is steadily losing influence in our neighborhoods, cities, and in the world. Churches struggle to remain relevant to a population that is more and more turned off by organized religion of any kind and especially the Christian faith. While social issues like the absent father in the home and the growing numbers of people living in poverty in our land are extremely important, perhaps the most pressing concern in America (and the world) is the lack of faith among our people.

Many people draw their views of the church from the mass media and Hollywood-types who portray Christianity in the most negative ways. These voices say: "there's no such thing as absolute truth and people who talk about absolutes are bigots". Christians are viewed as intolerant, close-minded, warmongers, and dangerous. Religion, in general, must be avoided or better still, stamped out.

What can we, as believers, do to reverse this devastating trend? In short, the church must change. Let me offer my own thoughts and, no, this isn't about how to set up visitation or making sure we greet guests and follow up after the fact. These are far more fundamental.

- Stop trying to "out-Hollywood" Hollywood. The programming has become the message in many contemporary churches. Most church-goers, especially the young people that are being solicited by these fellowships, are tech savvy individuals. Their lives are surrounded with touch screen, high definition, and instantaneous information. Too often the church attempts to make its production the centerpiece of worship. The significance of the gospel is lost in the glitter. There is nothing innately wrong with technology and it certainly can aid the worship experience. Use it as a tool to spread the gospel message.

- Make the Bible the foundation of all music. Secular music played and sung at high volumes doesn't honor God because there is no praise directed to our Lord and Savior. While entertainment has some value to a generation of people used to instant gratification, entertainment sours quickly and the message is eternal. Encourage worship leaders to make sure everything that is sung, whether choruses, hymns, or anthems are inspired by Scripture. It should also be noted that verses 1, 2, and 4 from the hymn book don't always have to be sung the same way every time. It's actually OK to bring new music into the church. And if the music is a little fast or a little loud today and it honors God, it should be welcomed into the church.

The style of worship music is less important than what is communicated by the musicians.

- Sermons should always be Biblically based and focus on Jesus and His grace. The Holy Bible is a living document with every verse "breathed out by God and profitable for teaching, for reproof, for correction, and for training in righteousness ", 2 Timothy 3:16. Ultimately, Scripture is all about Jesus. Now the narrative today may be about Abraham, Joseph, Samson, David, or Jeremiah but all 66 books are bound together by the theme of God's redemption of humankind through Jesus Christ. Guided by the Holy Spirit with Scripture as the foundation, every sermon can be fresh, inspirational, and a learning experience for the listener. In fact, "The best sermons which we ever preach are those which are fullest of Christ." - C.H. Spurgeon

- Leave outside the church the practices of legalism and pettiness. Our Savior's most passionate indictments were to the Pharisees and Scribes, the religious leaders of His day. Their hypocrisy and narrow-mindedness drew the ire of our Lord on multiple occasions. These men added onerous laws to Scripture that were so restrictive that they were impossible to keep. Jesus told them in Luke Chapter 11: "But woe to you Pharisees! For you tithe mint and rue and every herb, and neglect justice and the love of God. These you ought to have done, without neglecting the others". They focused on trivialities and ignored the significance of God's grace. Don't allow your church to dictate a set of rules and condemn those who do not follow them. Yes, the church should preach righteousness and obeying God's commandments but not like this snippet I heard from the pulpit recently. In the middle of a tirade against the state's lottery as gambling, the preacher paused and said that a nursery down the street had been sold and was being converted to a store selling beer and wine. His point was that churches had stopped being a voice in the community and these vices were the result. I suspect there were more than a handful of people in that church that bought lottery tickets and occasionally drank beer and wine. Any visitor involved in either of those activities would have been put off by the venom expressed from the pulpit. If the church is to help win the world for Christ "whosoever will— may come" must be its theme.

• The church must strike a balance between being in the world but not of the world. Some churches look, sound, and feel so much like the world's entertainment places that there is no distinguishable difference. When the church is just like every-day life the message of Christ will not stand out. We are called to be different. Romans 12:2 says: "Do not be conformed to this world, but be transformed by the renewal of your mind, that by testing you may discern what is the will of God, what is good and acceptable and perfect." In Ephesians 1:4 Paul says: "even as he chose us in him before the foundation of the world, that we should be holy and blameless before him." Christians are called to live holy, sanctified, different lives be-fore the world. But we are also called to go into the world. Our Lord said in Matthew 28:19: "Go therefore and make dis-ciples of all nations, baptizing them in the name of the Father and of the Son and of the Holy Spirit." The commandment is not to wait until the world comes into our building and then evangelize. We are to go into the world but not be conformed to the world. What is the answer to this conundrum? We must not withdraw from the world; instead make a difference in the world by living under the Lordship of Christ in everything that we do. So while we are mixing and mingling with the world's people, places, and things we should own different priorities, motives, and goals. In summary, we are in the world everyday caring and loving those who are on the journey with us but are not afraid to be viewed as being different.

• Teach what the Bible says, not what we wish it says. Scripture has some difficult passages to believe and accept. But, most people want the genuine article when it comes to faith. That means accepting even those verses that are counter-culture and uncomfortable. Some churches refuse to talk about hell believing it drives people away from the fellowship. Others deny that Christ is the only way to God. Still others tone down or avoid the reality that absolute truth exists in this world. Some call sin by another name (e.g. a psychological problem, a lack of self-esteem, a bad habit, or an educational deficiency). Many do not address tough social issues such as homosexuality, abortion, divorce, alcoholism, and the absent father for fear of offending some of the congregants. However, the Bible is the inspired Word of God. The world has questions and Scripture has the answers. By ignoring, disbelieving, or hiding part of what God has for us, people suffer.

• Demand excellence from the church staff. Let me say at the outset that I'm aware that there are no perfect people. I understand that personalities are different, as are counseling and teaching skills, educational backgrounds, and practical experience. I'm not talking about any of those. Let's first talk about preaching. I can't count the number of sermons I've heard in my life that were warmed over, preached many times before by the same man. The speaker looks as bored as some of the listeners. Time is too precious and the Bible is too rich to repeat worn out phrases. Added to that, we should expect more than tradition, clichés, and heartwarming tales to be the main dish of each sermon. Expect your pastor to dig deep into the Word when he prepares his message to bring nuggets of gold to the service every Sunday. When a pastor is discussing doctrine and states "the Bible says" expect to hear the exact chapter and verse where he is getting his information. Too often words flow from the pulpit with the prefix "the Bible says" when it is nothing more than someone's opinion. What about the staff in general? They must first love God with all their heart, soul, mind, and strength. They must then genuinely love people, all people. That means love God and other people more than programs or philosophies or buildings or, especially, more than "the way we've always done it." When those priorities are in order, excellence will be the hallmark of the staff.

The only hope for America and the world is Jesus Christ. Not education, not wealth, not politics, not government, not embracing the culture, or anything that only has temporal value. And where better than the church can people find what they need most? Paul said in 1 Corinthians 1:20-21: "Where is the one who is wise? Where is the scribe? Where is the debater of this age? Has not God made foolish the wisdom of the world? For since, in the wisdom of God, the world did not know God through wisdom, it pleased God through the folly of what we preach to save those who believe." What the church should be preaching and teaching is exactly what the world needs.

Churches in America and the world are dying a slow, painful death. God will retain a remnant to do His work on this earth. But it is not too late for Christians to wake up and restore the church to greatness. We must if we are to obey the great commission.

CHAPTER 9

GOD COMMANDS US TO FAST TOGETHER

Through the years I have attended many churches that strongly endorsed fasting, usually during a fundraising event. The idea of fasting is almost always presented as giving up specific foods or all food for a designated period of time. Cleverly named campaigns designed to open the congregation's purse strings for a building program are often intermingled with calls for prayers and fasting among the membership. Sacrifice is usually the foundation of every successful campaign with a call for each member to go "above and beyond" the tithe to help the church reach some designated goal. The sacrifice in many cases is more than financial. Often church members are asked to offer their time, talents, and resources to further the cause. Always there is a spiritual commitment to stretch the believer's faith to a greater closeness with God. Weekly there will be a testimonial by a member of the church expressing the sacrifices he/she has made to make sure the church reaches their potential and provides for the future generation. Testimonies usually have comments about the many meals that have been missed and the money that would have been spent on food was given to the program. I've even heard comments made that physical illness resulted because of the willingness of a church member to fast over a long period of time. But the closing remarks are that it was worth it to make sure that future generations will have a comfortable place to worship.

Another church I visited for a few months was having severe financial problems. Each week one of the congregants would stand before the gathering and talk about the sacrifice he or she had made to give extra during the crisis period. It seems that each week the fasting and sacrifice was greater than the week before. Several times the designated speaker talked about being physically ill because of the lack of sustenance and the strain that the financial burden on the church was placing on the individual.

Some evangelical churches call for a fast among all members on an annual basis. This practice can be as a sign of remorse for sin among God's people, to prepare for a new year of service by purging the body of harmful poisons, or simply to become a stronger Christian as the Bible seems to imply of a person who fasts.

Other reasons I've seen offered for a church wide fast are:

a) The church is about to make a major decision usually about staff or priorities.

b) The church has been in conflict and hurt feelings abound. Fasting becomes a sign of unity.

c) The church is sending a group on the mission field and asks for prayer and fasting for the success of the travelers.

d) The church has gained no new members in weeks or months and the leadership wants God's hand back on the fellowship.

e) To unify the fellowship as all participate in fasting together for a common cause.

Certainly there are plenty of other reasons that churches call for a fast among members. The practice is almost always brought up so God will answer a particular prayer and that fasting is spiritually beneficial. But what does the Bible say about fasting and especially about fasting when directed by church leadership?

First and foremost, the Bible does not command anyone ever to fast by not eating food. This is true both in the Old Testament to the Hebrew nation and to the Christian church of the New Testament. While the Old Testament law enumerated certain foods that should be eaten and others that should be avoided, there was never a direct command to fast. Leviticus 16:29-31 reads "And it shall be a statute to you forever that in the seventh month, on the tenth day of the month, you shall afflict yourselves and shall do no work, either the native or the stranger who sojourns among you. For on this day shall atonement be made for you to cleanse you. You shall be clean before the Lord from all your sins. It is a Sabbath of solemn rest to you, and you shall afflict yourselves; it is a statute forever." Instead of "afflict yourselves" in the ESV, the NIV reads "deny yourselves", the KJV says "afflict your souls" and the NASB has "humble your souls." God never said to go without eating; instead He commanded His people to deny themselves on the Day of Atonement which would mean to reject pleasures in many ways.

Some say that Zechariah 8:19 commands fasting: "Thus says the Lord of hosts: The fast of the fourth month and the fast of the fifth and the fast of the seventh and the fast of the tenth shall be to the house of Judah seasons of joy and gladness and cheerful feasts. Therefore love truth and peace." On the contrary, the Lord is commenting on the tradition (not commandment) of fasting in the fourth, fifth, seventh, and tenth months as a time of joy, gladness and cheerful feasts. One chapter earlier God asked His people: "4 Then the word of the Lord of hosts came to me: 5 'Say to all the people of the land and the priests, When you fasted and mourned in the fifth month and in the seventh, for these seventy years, was it for me that you fasted? 6 And when you eat and when you drink, do you not eat for yourselves and drink for yourselves?'" God reminded His people their traditions were not honoring Him.

Others say that fasting is commanded by God because of three verses as quoted in the King James Version of the Bible: Matthew 17:21 reads in the KJV: "Howbeit this kind goeth not out but by prayer and fasting." There is no verse 21 in the ESV or the NIV and the NASB cautions the reader that "early manuscripts do not contain this verse." It is possible that 16th century scribes added this language for the KJV. Another verse in the KJV is Mark 9:29: "'And he said unto them, This kind can come forth by nothing, but by prayer and fasting.'" But look at the ESV: "'And he said to them, "This kind cannot be driven out by anything but prayer."' Again the word fasting does not appear in the original language. Finally, 1 Corinthians 7:5 in the KJV: "Defraud ye not one the other, except it be with consent for a time, that ye may give yourselves to fasting and prayer; and come together again, that Satan tempt you not for your incontinency." The same verse in the ESV: "Do not deprive one another, except perhaps by agreement for a limited time, that you may devote yourselves to prayer; but then come together again, so that Satan may not tempt you because of your lack of self-control." The word fasting was apparently added by translators during the Middle Ages for that word is not part of the oldest and best manuscripts.

Still, though not commanded by God, Scripture does mention fasting by both the Israelites and the Christian church. In the Old Testament:

- Moses said "I neither ate bread nor drank water" for forty days both before and just after he received the "two tablets of the covenant" in Deuteronomy 9.

- In the Book of Samuel, David fasted for seven days after Nathan the Prophet exposed his sin with Bathsheba in an attempt to save the life of the young child born out of that illicit relationship.

- King Jehoshaphat ordered a fast among the people as he "was afraid and set his face to seek the Lord" when the enemies of Judah attacked the nation.

- The prophet Joel ordered the nation to "consecrate a fast" in an attempt to avoid God's judgment.

- Queen Esther asked the Jews in Persia to fast for three days and to pray for her safety before she went in uninvited to the King which could result in her death sentence.

God honored some of these fasts and others went for naught. In every case, the individual chose the action for a specific purpose; it was not commanded by God.

Likewise in the New Testament:

- Anna, the prophetess, who proclaimed the baby Jesus as the long-awaited Messiah, "did not depart from the temple, worshiping with fasting and prayer night and day" in the Book of Luke.

- In the Book of Acts Saul, later Paul the apostle, fasted for three days after his conversion experience on the Damascus road as he sought God's will for his life.

- Twice in the Book of Acts, the early church was said to be praying and fasting.

- Jesus Himself fasted for forty days in the wilderness before He began His earthly ministry in earnest. This is the only place in the New Testament that mentions Jesus fasting and was most likely a matter of necessity because there would have been nothing to eat in that place. Indeed Jesus said in Matthew 11:19: "The Son of Man came eating and drinking, and they say, 'Look at him! A glutton and a drunkard, a friend of tax collectors and sinners!' Yet wisdom is justified by her deeds." Apparently fasting was not a normal part of the Lord's routine.

God Himself directly addresses fasting in Isaiah Chapter 58. The Jews asked the Father a question in verse 3a: "Why have we fasted, and you see it not?" God answers in verses 3c and 4: "Behold, in the day of your fast you seek your own pleasure, and oppress all your workers. Behold, you fast only to quarrel and to fight and to hit with a wicked fist. Fasting like yours this day will not make your voice to be heard on high." God then goes on to explain what fasting should be. Read with me verses 6 and 7 of Chapter 58:

6 "Is not this the fast that I choose:
to loose the bonds of wickedness,
to undo the straps of the yoke,
to let the oppressed go free,
and to break every yoke?

7 Is it not to share your bread with the hungry
and bring the homeless poor into your house;
when you see the naked, to cover him,
and not to hide yourself from your own flesh?"

God makes clear in this directive that true fasting, a fast that pleases Him, is not about avoiding food. Instead, it is about denying ourselves and serving others. Jesus in Luke 9:23 said to be a true follower one must "deny himself and take up his cross daily." Christ also speaking in Matthew 22:36-40 when asked about the greatest commandment: "'Love the Lord your God with all your heart and with all your soul and with all your mind.' This is the first and greatest commandment. And the second is like it: 'Love your neighbor as yourself.' All the Law and the Prophets hang on these two commandments." It is simple and yet profound. To fast is to obey the two greatest commandments: Love God, Love Other People. But the most important and relevant teaching in the Bible about fasting came from Jesus Himself in the Sermon on the Mount. In Matthew 6:16-18 our Lord said: 16 "And when you fast, do not look gloomy like the hypocrites, for they disfigure their faces that their fasting may be seen by others. Truly, I say to you, they have received their reward. 17 But when you fast, anoint your head and wash your face, 18 that your fasting may not be seen by others but by your Father who is in secret. And your Father who sees in secret will reward you." Jesus made it clear that fasting is a private matter. If you as a believer choose to fast before God for whatever reason it should be between you and the Father. Nobody should know that you are fasting and, in fact, Jesus warned that others should not see or know you are fasting. Groups, families, and churches should not be making public that they are fasting. People who go before the church and talk about their personal discomfort or sacrifices they are making because of fasting stand in stark contrast to the Lord's specific instructions.

Finally, should you choose to fast, make sure none of these are the reason you are doing so:

a) To change the mind of God. Some people use fasting to get God to do what they want. Who can advise an immutable, sovereign God?

b) To appear more spiritual than other Christians. As already stated fasting is not a medal of superiority for any person.

c) To consider it a form of punishment for our sin. Jesus paid the debt for all of our sin and fasting should never be to castigate oneself for real or perceived wrongdoings.

d) To get closer to God or to make God notice us. We are not made more valuable in the eyes of God when we fast. Our Father is lovingly aware of His children and their needs at all times.

If fasting were necessary for spiritual growth God most assuredly would have commanded it. We should be careful not to mimic the Pharisees and Scribes of Jesus day when we choose traditions over commandments. Fasting is never presented as going without food anywhere in the Bible. Instead, fasting is denying oneself for the benefit of other people. Choosing to fast in this way is certainly not wrong if it done as Jesus instructed in the Sermon on the Mount.

CHAPTER 10

THE BIBLE IS RELEVANT IN OUR HOMES TODAY

The Holy Bible is the most beloved, most purchased, most power-ful, most hated, most ignored, most controversial book ever written. As divisive as it is inspirational, mysterious as it is enlightening, and as tedious as it is compelling, the Bible is a study in contrasts. So simple a child can understand its message yet so complex it confounds the brightest minds on the planet. And as many questions as the Bible an-swers will be the questions that are derived from its words. The books that make up the true canon of Scripture can stir the imagination and emotions of every reader. It is filled with heroes doing mighty deeds, miracles, mysteries, love stories, and action/adventure tales that stag-ger the imagination.

The Bible is not simply a book. Instead it is 66 books written by more than three dozen authors over a 1500 year period in three dif-ferent languages. The Scripture was written by a variety of authors that included kings, fishermen, tax collectors, doctors, prophets, and shepherds. God used these authors, most of whom never knew any of the other authors, to weave a remarkable tapestry of truth. Amazingly, all of these books are tied together with one central theme—God's redemptive plan for all people. Through its history, poetry, wisdom, prophecy, letters, and eye-witness accounts, the Bible is God's word to humankind.

I believe that the Bible is the inspired, holy word of God. It is inerrant, infallible, and immutable. Inerrant means without error in form or content. I believe it is the universal way in which God reveals Himself to human beings. Every word is important (especially the original languages of the scripture) and is inspired by God. This makes the Bible unique from any other book ever written. It is, by definition, absolute truth. I do not believe hymns or Christian songs are without error. Likewise the writings of theologians are not divinely inspired to be perfect. But God gave us Scripture exactly the way He wanted us to have it, no more and no less. Understand this carefully: not every question we have will be answered by Scripture in this lifetime. With that said, we as believers need to be careful not to add to the Word of God to justify our doctrine, conviction, creed or ideology.

Along with its inerrancy, the Word of God is infallible. This means that the truths of Scripture will never fail. The promises of God remain the same from generation to generation. We can depend on the writings of the Bible to help us develop our lifestyle, choose our career, build our family, decide on our church affiliation, and even form our politics. The Bible should be taught to our children and grandchildren and talked about wherever we are and to whomever we meet in life.

Immutable means the truth of the Bible is never changing. We can trust that what was once wrong is still wrong; what was once right is still right. Furthermore, it is ageless. Despite dramatic changes in our culture, education, wealth, and knowledge through the centuries, the Word of God is still important, up-to-date, and perfectly suited for this generation and every other. The Scripture can still be relied upon to be the foundation of every life because it is the same yesterday, today, and forever.

Most people would agree with everything I've said so far. An unscientific poll taken on the streets of most towns and cities in America with this question "Is the Bible the inspired Word of God?" would generate an overwhelming "YES" response by a vast majority of participants. Almost every household in the USA has at least one Bible and most have many copies. But in the same unscientific poll ask a second question, "Do you read the Bible regularly?" and the "YES" response would be vastly different. This generation of believers is classically illiterate of the teachings of Scripture. The Bible may be the single most ignored item in the home.

Each year, the Bible (published in many forms and translations) is always Number 1 on bestseller lists across the USA. It is more accessible now to the general populace than at any point in history. Anyone with an Internet connection can get 10 different versions of the Scripture with just a few keystrokes. The Bible has been translated into hundreds of dialects and is sent around the world by numerous organizations. It is called the Holy Word of God by most evangelicals and who wouldn't want to hear a word from God? Clearly, the Bible is readily available to almost anyone wanting to read it.

And yet, most people in the world know little to nothing about this great book. Most know that it is a "religious" book; some know that it is about God, and a few may know the Bible talks about Jesus. Even believers, frequent church goers, in general depend on a speaker (evangelist, priest, pastor, Sunday school teacher etc.) to tell them what the Bible says. There are dozens of different denominational groups, each with their own doctrines and belief systems. All claim to have the Bible as the foundation of all their teaching.

I find the responses interesting when I ask a believer what the Bible says on a certain topic. With few exceptions, the answer I get is "Well, Dr. *** says….." or "I heard my preacher say ….." or "< TV or radio speaker (you choose the name)> says ….."

This is a frightening and dangerous situation. Tune in to any "Christian" television or radio station and listen carefully to the messages presented. About one-half day is all you will need to be thoroughly confused as to what the Bible really says about most subjects.

So those who tell you the Bible is relevant in our society today are sadly mistaken. Of all the words used about Scripture such as inerrant, infallible, immutable, and inspired the most important should be relevant. However, most people, even those who claim to be Christ followers, do not ever read their Bible. Never, nada, none, zero, naught, it simply doesn't happen. Oh we may read the occasional Bible story to our children or grandchildren and we may even follow along on Sunday when the minister reads a passage. But how many times a week does the average Christian open the Word of God and with a prayer on his lips for discernment really read the Bible? We are a busy society with demands on our time from work, school projects, children's sporting events, social occasions with friends, doctor and dental visits, house cleaning, car repairs, and yes even church responsibilities along with dozens more. We simply don't have time to read God's word. So we depend on our pastor, Sunday school teacher, or the occasional TV preacher to teach us what the Bible says.

Besides the busyness of life, why else does the Bible remain essentially unread? Some say "I'm already a Christian; I don't need to read the Bible." Another may add "the Bible is a rule book and I can't keep all those rules and regulations." A third person might offer "the Bible is OK for other people but it's not really for me." I've heard some offer this reason: "I can't understand the book with all of the Old English and it's thee and thou words. Someone else explains: "Preachers and teachers argue about the Bible all the time. If they disagree so much, how am I supposed to understand it?" Finally (and it's my favorite): "I've heard it all before." I'm sure you've heard these and many other excuses not to read the Bible.

Many of us have sung hymns that say "thy word is a lamp to my feet", "wonderful words of light" and "ancient words that are true changing me, changing you" all expressing the truth of the beauty and necessity of reading, believing, and following God's word. But after singing these words on Sunday, we too often leave the fellowship and forget the Bible until we return next week and do it all again.

But, ultimately, what does God say about reading Scripture? Listen to this:

- John 8:31-32 – "So Jesus said to the Jews who had believed him, 'If you abide in my word, you are truly my disciples, and you will know the truth, and the truth will set you free.'" There is a great debate among people today about the application of truth or whether absolute truth even exists. Absolute truth is an unalterable, universal, and permanent reality. Many hold to the thesis that everything of meaning and value begins with the individual. Existentialists teach that the meaning and passion of life flow through the experiences of each person. Some say truth is relative defined to each person by background, customs, and—dare we say it again—human experiences. Others say truth cannot be known. But Jesus says you can know truth, absolute truth, by reading, understanding, and living (abiding in) the Word of God.

- Matthew 4:4 – "But he (Jesus) answered, "It is written, 'Man shall not live by bread alone, but by every word that comes from the mouth of God.'" When Jesus was tempted in the wilderness He responded to Satan with that statement. What does it mean? We as human beings cannot live on food alone; we need the Word of God for sustenance.

- Romans 15:4 – "For whatever was written in former days was written for our instruction, that through endurance and through the encouragement of the Scriptures we might have hope." Paul wrote to the believers in Rome that if we are to have hope in this life it will be from the encouragement of the Bible. How will any person survive without hope?

- 2 Timothy 3:16-17 – "All Scripture is breathed out by God and profitable for teaching, for reproof, for correction, and for training in righteousness, that the man of God may be complete, equipped for every good work." God breathed out every verse in the Bible through His Holy Spirit. We can rely on Scripture to help us deal with every situation or crisis in our lives. It can teach us, make us whole, and prepare us for whatever God has in store for our future. Our only defense against doubt and heresy is a thorough understanding of the Word of God.

- Hebrews 4:12 – "For the word of God is living and active, sharper than any two-edged sword, piercing to the division of soul and of spirit, of joints and of marrow, and discerning the thoughts and intentions of the heart." Unlike any other document ever written, the Bible is a living, active word that is timeless, cross-cultural, and powerful now and forever. To know God more intimately requires reading His word. In short, it is not just the truth, IT IS TRUTH.

To fully understand the Bible and the richness and flow of what God is offering, all of Scripture must be considered. That means in the context in which it was written and not just small pieces that are divvied up in a sermon or book. To draw life-long spiritual conclusions based upon sermons or books without ever having read the Bible carefully is both risky and short-sighted. Even great sermons or books are intermingled with the author's comments and opinions and cannot offer the full essence of the Bible by itself. Let me give you an example of my point. A photograph is made of a certain road passing through a neighborhood. The houses are beautiful with well-kept landscaping and fresh paint on all of the exteriors. The person viewing this photograph would have a mental image of what this street looks like. Suppose instead that the photographer had taken pictures a few blocks down the same road. The photos might reveal something totally different. Buildings are shuttered and windows are shattered and graffiti shrouds all of the structures. Stolen cars sit on concrete blocks stripped to the frame. Less than a mile away a totally different view would be derived of that street if the photo had been taken there. What's my point? Choosing small glimpses of Scripture may yield a picture image the Father did not intend for us to hold onto. We may miss something important because we were looking at the wrong aspect. Something God hates we may never hear because the pastor or author was afraid of offending someone. Something God loves may also be missed because of the pastor's or author's prejudice. You understand the point. Read God's word in context all the way through.

Now let's talk about the practical advantages of reading God's Word. Number one, lives will be changed. I've watched criminals become model citizens by allowing Scripture to change priorities. The sick have been miraculously healed, people have been rescued from the most hopeless situations, and life suddenly has meaning and purpose when reading, believing, and following the precepts of the Bible. Number two, Scripture points us to God. The Bible is 66 books about God's plan to redeem humankind. We can personally know the Holy, Righteous God and Scripture tells us how. Number three, we grow spiritually. We grow closer to God when we commune with Him in His word. When we pray, we talk to God; when we study His word, He speaks to us. Number four, as mentioned earlier, the Bible is the book of hope. We can take comfort in today, tomorrow, and eternity when we place our faith and trust in Christ as directed by the Holy Scriptures. Lastly number five, when we read God's word and we meditate and ponder what we've been given, the result will be joy in life every day. Not necessarily happiness every day as happiness is related to happenings. Crises and events will come into our lives that will be painful and distressing and we certainly won't be happy. But we can still have joy, the peace and comfort of knowing we are safe in the arms of an all-powerful and all-knowing Heavenly Father.

In summary, all mainstream denominations, churches, para-church groups, and Christian organizations of which I'm aware affirms the Bible as God's word. The Bible is taught at all of these as having precedence over verbal prophecy (preaching), experience, miracles, and any man-made rules and regulations. If Scripture really is inerrant, infallible, immutable, and eternal as these organizations teach, why isn't the Bible the most important single document on earth to a believer? I fear most professing believers don't really believe what their church says about this subject.

Let's face it. The only decision you will ever make in life that will have eternal significance is what you believe about Christ. In a hundred years the only person who will remember your name, know where you lived, what education you had, the number of children you sired, and know the name of the person you married will be someone doing an ancestry tree. It won't be important what your career was, how attractive you looked, or even what marvelous acts of mercy you performed for charity. While all of those things are important and should never be neglected, ultimately your decision about Christ is all that matters for the future. The Bible tells us how to have eternal life, to live a life full of joy, and how to be the very best person possible in the eyes of God. Isn't this worth making the Bible relevant?

CPSIA information can be obtained at www.ICGtesting.com
Printed in the USA
LVOW120154130313

323926LV00001B/72/P

9 781478 715481